# RURAL HOME

## Reflections and Recollections

Bonnie U. Holland

 www.trafford.com

**North America & international**
toll-free: 1 888 232 4444 (USA & Canada)
phone: 250 383 6864 ✦ fax: 812 355 4082

# TABLE OF CONTENTS

# DEDICATION

To my husband, Gene Sykes, who

Makes me laugh,

Makes me rest,

Taught me to crossword,

Does housework,

Brings me special treats,

Is the best errand guy in the world,

Helps me do everything,

Has changed my life in ways I never dreamed possible,

Is the very best!

# RURAL HOME

By reading my memoirs, *Rural Home*, I hope you will learn from my mistakes and at the same time gain some insights into living well. My journey has been interesting and sometimes painful. But now that I'm at Rural Home, it is exactly where I want to be. Sophisticated country living gives me great joy and freedom. When I leave this place I hope to have ten toes up and set out on an even more glorious journey!

To protect the innocent and the guilty, names of some characters and locations have been changed. Those who know me well will recognize the stories but few will know where fact ends and fiction begins. There is a thread of truth throughout Rural Home. Anyone taking offense to what I have written and who recognizes himself/herself must know that I say all that to say this, "If the shoe fits, wear it".

# PURPOSE

I regret that I cannot begin to name all the people who deserve acknowledgement for their impact on my life. Freshest in my mind are the many friends who gave generously of their time and talents while this work was in progress. My dear husband, Gene Sykes, cheered me on from start to finish, and is to whom this memoir owes its existence. His love, support, cooperation, and abiding belief in my work allowed me to begin and complete this first edition of my memoirs. He has extended, enriched, and balanced my life in countless ways.

Special thanks also go to Dr. Katrina Smith who never let me forget, even for a moment, that I should be writing every day.

Our chosen grandchildren, Brandon and Jenny Langford, shared their time and talents typing and technically enhancing this writing.

Some of my present and former friends have given me great insights into life and to the true nature of relationships. God allows others to come into (and to go from) our lives as our needs demand. Some of those who I felt would be my friends forever really never were.

Truth-telling, the heart of many subjects is a central challenge in my life. "Truth-telling" is much more encompassing and courageous than "honesty". By uncovering my true self I am no longer whispering but shouting out loud. I refuse to pretend anymore. In my past and in some of yours, pretense was, on occasion, necessary for survival. What follows are my reflections on my life and the lives of some others who have so greatly impacted my journey. My hope is that you will join me in examining how we all engage in deception and approach truth-telling which is at the heart of who we are in this world and what kind of world this really is.

1

Self-awareness and introspective reasoning make me think about what really matters in my life. The reconciliation of what is, what was, what might have been and what is yet to come has been a true awakening for me.

As I grow older I don't regret many of the things I did in my life. I only regret occasions and possibilities I didn't embrace! I now know that God's unprecedented favor makes dreams come true.

There are no learned skills that can substitute for the feeling of having a lot to say, of sharing news. Writing this memoir has been a type of confessional for me. Some of what I've written has been painful to remember and after examining my conscience, I realized that I could not have friends or family looking over my shoulder. This has been my search for truths from which I ran for many years. But now, this is my way of dealing with memories, impressions and emotions which had some control over me. After confronting them they hold little power over me. By honestly sharing what I think, feel and have survived, I hope that someone will get the wisdom and benefit of my experiences without having to live it.

The most difficult part of writing has been deciding what to leave out. The memories and moments I've been scribbling about for years are now in print. All of us are full of contradictions and conflict and have evolved out of our many different selves. This has been my opportunity to explore how I have become who I am today. Hopefully, some of this will help you know how I got here from there. I really don't know if I'm wiser than I was yesterday. I only hope that I'm still learning every day. Sometimes what I don't say is an opening for you to express your own truth, either verbally or by actions and/or reactions.

No matter where we are in our life we must be there totally and feel everything completely—even pain. Healing takes much less time when we allow ourselves to *feel* rather than *fill* the moments.

The intent of my life is to do my very best in all that I attempt and to be used for a higher purpose than myself. Allowing myself to *go with the flow* opens portals I never knew existed.

Even when we feel blocked or controlled by circumstances we still have the option of beginning a meaningful journey. Seizing opportunities that present themselves can lead to the fulfillment of our dreams. By setting our hearts free, breaking a few rules, disrupting the system and even being a bit socially inappropriate, we can rock boats. When we become true to ourselves, we no longer need the acceptance of others. If we never speak our deepest truths we will refuse to hear our own souls. When our lives are shared by fear, steered by social expectation or stalled by conflicting demands, we are the only ones who can free our hearts.

Our inner voices, the ones we have ignored most of our lives, when heeded, will provide clarity to our emotions and reactions. Everything will fall into place. Journaling provided me a wonderful confidante and gave meaning to my being until I was ready to share my life with others.

When I hid my truths, my heart would, from time to time, shock me, almost like a disobedient child. It would have tantrums and/or pity parties and I was invited to both. When my feelings were repressed they would burst out in sometimes unhealthy ways. By following my heart and freeing my imagination, my life has taken me to places I could never have imagined. My life has been filled with enough love to share with many. Following my heart has allowed me to leave footprints and fingerprints on many who have entered my life. I am to the point in my life where there are many more yesterdays than tomorrows, yet, I wake up each day, happily anticipating today's joys. I've learned that the bigger my problem, the brighter my future.

Each of us has been called on to start a new life after a frightening diagnosis, a marriage break-up, loss of a job . . . and we are driven to be hopeful, full of a God-given resilience which is surely a basic human instinct. And each time, we arrive on the other side of life's deepest abyss, a wiser, stronger, more empathetic person. God's challenges to us can become our greatest gifts. For those who live in the past, these wonderful experiences and spurts of growth are lost forever. I have always lived with the belief that *whatever happens, happens for the best*. We must find that best by constantly living life to its fullest and enjoying every minute as though it could be our last. The *what if* in life must become *what is* in order for us to grow to our fullest potential. It is not the distance, but the direction we travel that counts. Discipline determines our destiny.

# CHILDHOOD MEMORIES

My dad and I had so much fun together. I, and everyone else, knew I was his favorite child. My husband tells me often that he is finishing the job of *spoiling* which my father began a long time ago. Saturday nights were *date nights* for us and bring to mind many of my favorite childhood memories. I have lived long enough that many of the stores and small businesses in my hometown no longer exist. One such was the 'Duck In' which was a very small diner with three or four tables and chairs along the outside wall and a long sit-down bar in its middle. The two prettiest teenagers in town served as waitresses and after all the other businesses on that block closed on Saturday nights, they offered curb service as well. Mine was a very standard order—a hamburger and Dr. Pepper or sometimes a cherry Coke. After Daddy and I finished our sandwiches, we would park a couple of blocks up the street to *people watch*. This is still a favorite past-time for me. I am always more interested in fact than fiction and human beings do say and do the darndest things.

Often times, Daddy and I would go to Montgomery and our favorite haunt there was Chris's Hotdog Stand. Daddy was a very tall, big man and ten or twelve of those hotdogs was just a good meal for him. I don't remember the price of those dogs by the time he and I would go there but he loved to recount that he had been eating at Chris's since they were priced at a nickel each.

The Ice Capades and South Alabama Rodeo were annual treks for us. Only in my dreams am I as graceful as those beautiful girls on ice skates! But I can dream still. Daddy loved to tell that I never *wanted* anything; I always *needed* whatever that was. When I was about four, I decided I wanted a big white cowgirl hat. When he inquired about the price, it was a bit more than he felt justified to spend. But, in order to encourage him to change his mind, I seated myself on the concrete bleacher directly behind him, constantly bumping him with my foot and saying with every breath, "I want that hat!" After about an hour of aggravation he decided the price of that hat would be a bargain if he could have some peace and quiet.

When I was in first grade my best friends' names were Judy Lane and Forest Lane, Lane being their middle given names. I did not understand nomenclature at that time and wanted to be 'Bonnie Lane'. At that young age, I tried to do everything like my same-named friends. Peer pressure, for the only time I can remember, was alive and well. They came to school after Christmas holidays with matching shoes. My parents always took my sisters and I to Montgomery to be fitted with very expensive shoes, but that mattered not to me. After a couple of days of looking at their shoes I decided to tear the heel off one of my shoes so I would *need* shoes just like theirs. At recess, the three of us used a rough piece of metal on the playground to work the heel of my right shoe loose. When we returned to the classroom, my teacher sent me to the office to phone my parents to come get me because my shoe was torn up. Daddy was the available parent that day and had a hard time understanding how that practically new, expensive shoe had lost its heel. He took me straight to the local shoe shop to have that heel re-attached. When he put my shoe back on I was sure I could not walk on that foot; something was still very wrong with my shoe. He nor the cobbler could feel anything inside the shoe that should be hurting my foot. After several minutes of my masquerade, he decided to waste no more of the store owner's time and said we'd just have to buy another pair of shoes. I went directly to the pair I wanted, he paid for them and I walked out of that store in shoes just like my friends were wearing. On the way back to school, I could not help saying, "I now have shoes just like Judy Lane and Forest Lane". I think my father was so amused and amazed at me that I received no much needed discipline for my deception. Until his death, he enjoyed telling the shoe story.

My dad would smoke a pipe occasionally and we children had seen him clean and oil the bowl of his beautiful pipe which he had brought back from Europe. We rarely touched it because we knew it was special to him. It was always in its rack on the table by his chair in the living room. We girls were taught from a very early age how to clean the house and on one Saturday morning we were helping Mother get the house ready for some special company. One of my sisters decided we should be really good cleaners and oil Daddy's pipe as we had seen him do. The only 'oil' we saw close by was in the Vicks Vaporub jar. We took turns rubbing that greasy substance into every nook and cranny of the pipe and then took turns wiping it very, very clean. We were sure Daddy would be so proud of us. And he was, until he lit his pipe. I still remember how he coughed, spit, sputtered, and spewed some obscenities! He was not pleased!

After my sisters graduated high school and went away to college, I became chief cook and bottle washer, so to speak. During the summer, I did most of the grocery shopping, meal planning, cooking, and general housekeeping. I always created projects for myself such as painting a room, creating a new flower bed, or some sewing project. We had a screened-in back porch which extended the full width of our house. We had several chairs, a couple of tables, and three swings on that porch. In the afternoons when Daddy came home from work, he'd come in the back door, go directly to shower, and after his bath would put on khakis or pajama bottoms and a t-shirt. We usually had an early dinner and his day was not complete until he sat in his favorite swing and read the newspaper—every word of it. I had decided to take on a very ambitious project and repaint the back porch. To really spruce it up, I decided the wooden swings needed repainting as well. Mother and I had taken down the swings, leaving their metal chains in place, and put them on work horses in the shed so I could paint them the next morning. As was Daddy's habit, he picked up his newspaper and was reading the headlines as he walked to his favorite place on the porch. He would always slide his hand down the chain as he lowered himself directly onto the swing. This particular day he slid his hand and his body all the way to the floor in one swell poof! He was not extremely happy about my latest project and stated that his swing needed to be re-hung by the time he got home the next day. When Mother and Daddy moved back to the farm, many years later, that swing was still hanging right there.

My mother and daddy had to have loved each other. They were truly like oil and water, never mixing very well. He always voted Republican, she Democrat. He loved to eat and loved good food more than anyone I've ever known while Mother only ate to live. They always had separate bank accounts. She was always cold-natured and he was always warm-natured. One year for Christmas, I gave them a dual controlled electric blanket, hoping they both would be more comfortable. Things went well for the first few days with the new blanket but when Mother changed the linens she inadvertently reversed the controls. As Daddy would tell this story, that night the temperature was in the teens. Mother continued to complain that she was freezing and Daddy kept throwing the covers back because he was so hot. He had her control and she had his. They discovered Mother's error about daylight, only after they had kept each other awake all night.

My mother's parents lived a couple of miles from us when we were young children. The school bus route was such that the driver could drop us at our house or theirs. So my sisters and I spent a lot of time with them. My grandfather was one of the finest men I've ever known. For as long as I can remember he taught Sunday School, was song leader at his church and never missed a service. And he lived such a good life as well. He was always a good neighbor and shared his time and talents with everyone. He treated my grandmother like the Queen she thought she was. He never said a harm word about anyone. He had a very deep and abiding faith in God but he knew God's power as well, especially when it came to bad weather. I remember being awakened many nights from a deep sleep and being told to go to the storm pit. The storm pit was located across the red clay road which, when wet, was obstacle enough to deter the faint of heart. When bright strikes of lightning were illuminating the sky and ground, I would wonder if I wouldn't be safer to have stayed in bed. And then, when the first person got to the storm pit, they had to open the heavy wooden door to the earthen pit which was dug into the side of the hill, light the kerosene lanterns and candles, and check to see if there were any rattlesnakes under the seats, I was certain staying in bed would have been a better option. Not to mention the smell of mold and mildew and the numerous spiders who were ever present. I learned from the storm pit experience that sometimes the cure is much worse than the illness.

My love of nature has existed for as long as I can remember. One day when my grandfather came come for lunch after plowing one of his fields, he laid down on the front porch to stretch his back for a few minutes before having his meal. I usually met him as he approached the house with a glass of tea or ice water and we would visit while he rested his back. One day, a hummingbird kept flying around us and Papa picked up his hat and threw it at the beautiful creature. The hat landed brim down, flat on the porch floor, and the hummingbird was under it. He drilled tiny holes all around the top of Papa's hat before being released. Papa always told me that was his favorite hat because it was *air conditioned*.

I had the opportunity of growing up while being made to feel very loved and special by my parents, grandparents, aunts, and uncles. They all made me feel very special—so much so that I thought the people who sang on the radio were singing just for me. If the radio was on at home and I walked across the pasture to my Grandmother's to find her radio on, I was certain those singers had followed me and were inside my grandmother's radio, singing only for me! My optimistic ego developed very early in life.

My parents told that I started talking in complete sentences and always spoke like an adult. I have always loved learning new words and when I was in second grade, midget was one of those new words. We had two new girls who came to our school who were very petite, acrobatic dancers. I so wanted to be like them but I was always one of the tallest in my class and agility was not one of my gifts. One night at dinner I was telling my family about these new girls but got my words mixed up and said, "I want to be an idiot". My sister Julie assured me that I was and always would be. My entire family had a good laugh at my "idiocy".

My parents left my sisters and me home alone for a few minutes when I was about three. Julie decided we should play a new game she had made up called "Running Through the House With Eyes Closed". Since I was the youngest, I got the privilege of being first. I promptly ran into the door facing and still have a scar over my left eye which reminds me regularly of my stupidity and naiveté.

Any time my parents went out of town, they invariably returned with donuts. There was not a bakery in our small town so this was a real treat for us. If any of us had to go to the doctor in Montgomery, shopping or fun, the bakery in Normandale (the first shopping center I remember) was a definite stop on our list. My last birthday before my Dad (who was bedridden by that time) died, he sent Mother to get my donuts! I always preferred them to any birthday cake. My husband continues the tradition and knows exactly what it takes to make me feel better. I do not need them for my health but they always warm my heart and tummy. All is right with the world when I'm eating a warm, squishy, wonderfully fresh donut!

My dad and I used to go fishing regularly but all that ended when I was about fifteen. We would get the truck and boat packed and ready to travel the night before our trip to the lake so we could leave home way before daylight the next morning. We were fishing in a large pond that had many willow trees along its bank and jetties. We had found a really hot spot because the bream were bedding and we were catching fish almost as fast as he could take them off our hooks. Being the squeamish soul that I am, I would catch my cricket or worm with pliers and then thread my hook through what was remaining of the poor creature. I had little action on the end of my line but continued to fish anyway. I had hung my casting line in the willows a few times that morning and assumed I had done so again. I continued to pull and tell Daddy I was hung in a willow tree. When I looked at the blood streaming down my father's face, I was ready to be taken to the landing and home. I had caught him in the ear and continued to yank on that line until I lost the biggest, bloodiest, catch of the day! He never took me fishing again in a pond surrounded by trees—of any kind! My story is as close to truth as my memory serves me but Daddy's version of this was greatly exaggerated and much more entertaining.

During the summer between my twelfth and thirteenth year, I became friends with Lauren Jones. Her mother, father and younger sisters were my second family since I spent the night at her house or she at mine almost every night of that entire summer. Her mother was a delightful lady who never seemed to be rushed or busy. She had time to play games with us or just sit and talk for hours on end. Mrs. Jones read every word of the newspaper every day and clipped coupons before coupon clipping was in vogue. She never made a grocery list as did my mother but shopped only with her coupons. If it was not on sale, Mrs. Jones did not buy it. In the fifties, angel food cake was very popular and was on sale every week. Just as was macaroni and cheese, canned corn, bread (two loaves for a dollar) and potatoes. So, at meal time, the Jones had the same thing for lunch and dinner, every day of the week—corn, macaroni and cheese, mashed potatoes, bread, and of course, for desert, angel food cake!

Mr. & Mrs. Jones were very *round* and Lauren's little sister was the fattest girl in our school. I finally came to realize that just because it's on sale, it is not necessarily a bargain! Especially when it comes to carbohydrate laden foods! I must have had enough angel food cake to last me a lifetime because I almost never serve it.

Living in a small rural town while growing up had its advantages. Local gossip helped to dictate good behavior. But, there was little in the way of entertainment for teenagers. In those days, a group of us, boys and girls, would get together and *ride around*—no particular destination in mind. If we encountered another carload of teens we'd park on the street corner and talk for hours. A few of the crowd would become couples who dated but most of us were just friends with everyone. Neither the police nor parents had to worry about us because we were really good kids looking for company, not trouble.

One night, under a full moon, a group of us decided we were in the mood for watermelon. My uncle had a large field of watermelons so I suggested we go there to steal our treat. When that melon was finally broken into and the sweet flesh revealed, I could not eat a bite of it! My uncle would have given us a truckload of those melons had I asked for them. That watermelon is the only thing I've ever stolen. I could not wait for the light of day the next morning so I could go tell him what I had done. He made my guilt even stronger by not scolding me. Before I could get back to my parents to confess my sin to them, he had telephoned them to make sure they would not fuss at me. That sense of wrong has stayed with me since that very day. I think I learned my lesson well.

# BIG MAMA

Relationships with our mothers are never simple and there is a deep and inexplicable difference between us. Respecting our individual innate traits is necessary for a harmonious existence. There is an old saying which bears much truth: "If you want a guilt trip, just call your mother!"

Grandmothers, however, allow us to be ourselves totally and have such special places in our hearts that long after they're gone, a smell or a simple chore or a taste (or a taste we long for but can never duplicate exactly) will bring her dainty porcelain face, beautiful hands and feet to mind. She is here with me in a place she's never seen. She died when I was thirteen and she was eighty-three. She called for me to come to her bedside and gave me her gold wedding band, which I had been allowed to play with for as long as I can remember. I was her favorite grandchild and she was definitely my favorite grandmother. I have such fond memories of her and remember spending only quality time with her. She was my Dad's mother and lived across the pasture from our house. She was short, maybe five feet tall and very pleasingly plump. By today's standards, she was extremely voluptuous and always wore corsets and bras that looked downright painful to me. But everything had to be in its place and standing straight up and out. She always smelled good and had the most beautiful hands and feet I've ever seen—like those of an exquisite doll. Her breasts were so large that they got in her way. After lunch every day, she read the Montgomery Advertiser before our afternoon nap. It was my job to hold one edge of the paper while she held the other. She cooked lunch every day and fed the field hands as they came in from plowing or harvesting. I'm sure she did many things other than cooking lunch but in my child's mind, that's the only work I remember her doing. The maid was always there to clean up the kitchen and work in the house. She did not live in Big Mama's house but was always there—no matter if I spent the night or just dropped by for a hug and kiss.

Big Mama's hoe cake cornbread was better than any I've ever eaten and her rice pudding was divine. But in my mind, anything Big Mama did was perfect.

She and I would stroll around the yard every few days and she would make notes of what needed to be done. The next morning, those chores were accomplished by Beebee, her favorite laborer. Her yard was always kept to perfection—not a blade of grass anywhere. This was in the days when yards were swept, not raked. I have some of her milk and wine lilies growing here at Rural Home and when they bloom, I simply have to sniff them to stimulate the memory of my precious grandmother.

My uncle, Will Knight, married an older woman when he was only seventeen. But that union was very short-lived—my grandmother had that marriage annulled and he did not marry again until age fifty-two. He worked for the federal government as an FDA inspector and traveled extensively. There was a constant flow of correspondence between Big Mama and him. I loved his trips home because he was the uncle every girl wishes for. He spoiled me rotten and never forgot to bring me gifts. As he would be coming home, he always stopped by my school to see me and give me a gift. Imagine how special that made me feel. He was the uncle who would take me shopping for school clothes every year and I never remember his putting a limit on what I could spend. If I liked a garment and if it fit, he was happy to buy it for me. When I was twelve, he gave me a *princess ring* with real diamonds in it! Even though they were very small, they were diamonds after all!

My grandmother outlived seven husbands and had children only by the middle one-fourth from the last and fourth from the first. One baby daughter was still born and another daughter died at age two. My father and Will Knight were her surviving children and they were a handful.

Both of them were very spirited and were a bit wild in their younger years. I wish I had recorded the stories my Dad told about their youthful escapades.

Big Mama owned a good bit of real estate; it was inherited from her parents or her deceased husbands or that she bought on her own. Several of the older businessmen in Luverne, most of whom are now deceased, have told me stories about buying property from her.

She was a very good businesswoman who lived a simple life. As I look back on her life, I think my grandmother must have been very stable and happy. I never remember her raising her voice or displaying anger.

When I was about four years old, she and I took my first train ride to her friend's. We departed for Chatom, Alabama, in the morning and returned late that afternoon. She wanted me to have all kinds of experiences so we rode the bus to Montgomery one day, spent the night with her brother, Piney and his wife, Elizabeth, and returned home the next afternoon. On that particular trip, they took me to Oak Park and to the Elite Café for lunch. She knew how to make lasting memories and I realize now what a special grandmother she was.

For as long as I live and can think about my grandmother and uncle, there will be two special spots in my heart. I remember them every day, in a hundred ways. They are with me still.

# FORGIVENESS

When characters are so real and situations are so factual, we must view them with total honesty.

In order to love fully we must first appreciate our own inner beauty and learn to love ourselves. By embracing the lessons our history teaches us, we create an environment in which love abounds. Emotional healing frees us from guilt and grief and is a gift we owe ourselves. Unconsciously repressing our feelings tends to wreak havoc in our lives and on our health. I was an older woman by the time I married Gene and was able to freely expose some of my childhood wounds. His love, acceptance and trust have helped me begin to heal. Having him listen to my truths without being judgmental has opened my heart to many truths I wish I had been able to accept much earlier in my life.

At some point in my childhood I decided that exhibiting anger was shameful and that *appearances* were everything. I therefore pretended my homelife was peaceful and ideal. It was anything but. My sister Julie, who was three and a half years older than I, was the main character in my childhood memories. Had our relationship been anywhere near normal, she would have been my mentor and protector, but she was my persecutor. The only emotions I felt when in her presence were fear and dread. She delighted in hurting me physically but much more damaging was what I experienced mentally. I have anxiety attacks on occasion and each of those feels just like it felt when she would hold me tight and not allow me to move—not even an inch. Or when she would lock me in a closet, turn off the lights and go outside to catch a frog, cricket, or grasshopper; then crack the door and throw the critters on me. To this day, I cannot abide the thought of something crawling on me. The flashbacks are horrifying and I resist them on a regular basis.

A very vivid memory of her cruelty is the one when she lured me to the top of an eight-foot stack of lumber, crutches and all (I had come down with polio the prior year) and pushed me off. When Julie talked me into climbing onto the pile of lumber, I never dreamed that she would push me off. I remember what I was wearing—a simple little green and brown plaid skirted dress with a brown bodice and matching plaid binding at the neck and sleeves. We had had school pictures made that day. She and I were dressed alike. She had taken my crutches up the ladder for me so I could walk around on the stack of lumber. This felt like such a major feat for someone who had trouble walking—period. The next thing I remember was being crouched on the ground with her standing at the edge of the stack, waving one crutch in the air, laughing hysterically and telling me she had me where she wanted me. I do not remember how I got up from the ground or how I got home. I only remember that I had a black eye the next day.

No matter what discipline my parents meted out to her, her misbehavior only intensified. Since I had a physical handicap and she was very athletically inclined, we had little in common while growing up. I was very studious and quiet with a perfectionist personality. I would spend hours decorating the Christmas tree with each and every ornament placed for balance and beauty. In my youth, no tree was complete until it was adorned with tensile icicles. Julie would never help with the tedious job of hanging all the lights and ornaments but would always come through just as I was beginning to hang all those individual strings of foil. She would grab a handful of them and throw them at the tree. It was not possible to pick those globs out of the perfectly hung tree and therefore, I felt that the entire effort was for naught. She delighted in making a mess of anything I attempted to make perfect.

Even though she was three and a half years older than I, my parents made me help her with her school work. I could read her textbooks and then tutor her so that she could maintain grades good enough to be a cheerleader. I was called on to read my exceptionally written papers to the higher level classes and her particular class always seemed to be one of those. It angered her when her teachers would explain to her that she should apply herself as I did. None of them could have known the prices I paid for their remarks to her. Anytime she was nice or affectionate to me, I knew that her hidden agenda would soon reveal itself. If she came to snuggle in my bed, it usually was because she was positioning herself to hold me so tightly that I could not move, again, not even an inch. During my anxiety attacks, I always relive that exact feeling of hopeless helplessness. I pray daily that God will relieve me of this horrible memory and reaction.

My family truly put the *dys* in *dysfunction*! And all of us were involved in the elaborate cover-up to make us appear *normal* to the rest of the world. Excellence in certain areas of our lives—Julie's athleticism and cheerleading, Britt's beauty and 4-H Club accomplishments and awards and my excellent grades and creativity were felt to be adequate to compensate for any and all other shortcomings.

My father worked out of town for weeks at the time. Mother worked full time and we were left in the care of a live in maid. When Mother was home, she did her best to discipline Julie, but spanking, taking away privileges or even making her sit under the *snake tree* (a huge oak tree in the front yard in which we were sure snakes resided) were pitiful attempts at getting her attention. I now understand that my parents never identified her *currency* because nothing ever worked for more than a few brief moments.

When my sister Britt graduated high school and went away to nursing school, my entire family was saddened. When Julie finally decided to go away to school and no longer resided in our house, I felt a joyous relief. I never missed having my clothes taken without my permission, my treasures broken, my room trashed or my peaceful existence threatened.

When she would return home, even for very brief visits, utter chaos was the order of the day.

Motion sickness, especially car sickness has been the bane of my existence—forever. When I was a child, we never got into the car without a bag, a pan or some container and a wet towel because I almost always threw up any time I had to travel. I dared not get into the backseat because I'd vomit before we were out of the driveway. To this day, I ride in the driver's seat or the passenger's front seat and look straight ahead for the duration of a trip, whether short or long. My sister Julie always hated that I got to ride in the front seat (shotgun) as she called it. There was always the same uproar and chaos as we were loading into the car. I remember that she would run to the car, seat herself firmly in the front passenger's seat and cross her little arms across her chest as though she were ready to ride. Invariably, Mother or Daddy would be telling her to get in the back seat, she knew that I had to ride in the front seat and the furor would begin. Sometimes it would be just a simple sassiness to parental commands but more often than not, they would have to physically remove her from the front to the back, while she kicked, screamed, and cried. The tantrums lasted sometimes throughout the trip and through shopping, appointments or whatever was on the agenda for the day. I remember feeling sorry for her because she never got to enjoy anything! After years of reading self-help books and studying human nature, I now know that this was her choice. Her insatiable need for attention was ever present. My riding *shotgun,* as she called it, was just another reason for her innate dislike of me.

My sister Julie called recently to tell me I was on her *to do list*—just before mopping the kitchen floor! No joke! It would have made me feel really good had she said she was thinking about me or some such nicety but that would be way too much to expect. I must admit that I do not telephone her at all. However, I am always polite to her when she calls. The anxiety attacks are far fewer and less severe now that I am on medication. I wish now that I had begun therapy many years ago because I now know that the healing from such emotional trauma is very slow. I'm not yet sure that mine will ever be complete. I will continue to work on myself every day.

For most of my life, I never even discussed my painful memories of the abuse my sister gave me when we were children. After I began having very serious anxiety attacks, I knew that only I could find the source of them. I was, by that time, able to talk to my husband about any and everything so I began to share some of my childhood memories and experiences with him. As soon as I began putting into words my childhood experiences I began having fewer and less severe anxiety attacks. This was probably the impetus I needed to begin writing my Rural Home.

As I have written, read and discussed this very wide-spread problem, I now know that many, probably most, families have experienced similar sibling conflicts. I think I held all of this to myself and never even mentioned it to anyone except one of my mother's best friends. She has assured me that mother's recognition of this conflict existed but that she was ill-equipped to resolve it. Mother and I never discussed it. We only tried to live through it silently and alone. I do not fault my parents but do hope that other families who read this and see themselves in a similar situation will seek outside help much earlier than I did. Since I've been writing my memoirs, I have often wondered what Julie's reaction to this truth will be. We have both lived almost seventy years on this wonderful place called Earth but on entirely different levels.

I am not much of a dreamer because I'm not much of a sleeper (usually only 3 or 4 hours of sleep per night). If I dream, the ones I remember are, most of the time, beautiful, peaceful, happy dreams. But, recently, I had a very sleepless, dream-filled night, or more specifically, a nightmarish evening. I spent, what in my dreams seemed, the whole night running from my sister Julie who was hitting me every time she got close to me. Eventually, while panting for breath I pointed a fly swatter at her and told her that I was going to hurt her if she hit me again. We made eye contact and for the first time in my life (even if it was in a dream) I saw what I thought was fear in her eyes. When I awoke, I was gasping for breath and realized that she was no longer there. I could finally breathe normally! It was, after all, just a dream.

It has taken me a lifetime to find the right place in my heart and in my head for my very dysfunctional relationship with Julie. I cannot reconstruct the past but I am determined to forgive myself for being merely human and remembering it with searing clarity. I love her—simply because I'm supposed to love my sister. My friends, however, are my true *sisters*. They are the ones to whom I rush to tell good news and bad news as well. They truly share my life and no matter what, love me: weaknesses, imperfections and all. In my life today, I do everything in my power to make others feel loved and appreciated. I never received that from my biological sister Julie.

As I look back with informed adult eyes I realize that the only explanation for our total disconnect had to be based in the fact that she was a bully before bullying was in vogue. My parents, I'm certain, did everything possible to protect me but their efforts fell very short of my emotional needs. The fact that God made me the way he did—sensitive, serious-minded and generous made me defenseless against her strong, emotional terrorism. But, God made both of us just the way he intended. And put us together just the way He intended. I now know that He was molding me into the survivor that I have become.

By expressing my memories of my sibling's actions, I simply aim to help parents, help their children, and to do a better job of parenting these behaviors in their own families. And, my intent is not to hurt my sister in any way. To me, forgiveness was my first requisite for healing and my healing emotionally has become necessary. Thank God for giving my physician the ability to prescribe the appropriate medication, for giving my husband an ear of understanding, and for giving me a forgiving spirit. I wish for my sister the peace that I am finding as my healing continues.

Forgiveness takes place inside the individual who has a change of heart; not the one who is forgiven. Letting go of anger is good for the body and soul.

In essence, the ability to forgive means that we rise above the conflict as a way of taking care of ourselves. Pardoning someone's misbehavior does not mean that we condone their actions. It does not mean that we have let go of our opinions about another person's actions or attitudes. We simply release our frustration or sadness that is eating away at us. When we stop needing to be right it frees our energy so we can focus on the future.

Oftentimes, whatever made us angry or hurt our feelings is based on misunderstanding. The wrong appears to be far less significant if we consider that the offender didn't mean what we thought they meant. Forgiveness is a gift—both to the person who is forgiven but even more to the person who forgives.

When we forgive, we love. When we love, God shines his light on us.

Forgiveness can, and often does, open our hearts to be hurt again. If we risk closeness in relationships, we risk being hurt. But, while forgiving, we can protect ourselves from further pain by setting clear boundaries with equally clear consequences should those boundaries be violated.

Forgiveness can be one of the most difficult things we ever do. But, it can be one of the most worthwhile. Choosing to be *better*, not *bitter* is a good thing.

# ALLEN

I have learned that there are many types of love. My first love was the most sexual, lustful love of my life. Age and hormones played tremendous roles in my marriage to C. Allen Blackstock. He was a very intelligent young man who received an appointment to West Point after graduating from a small high school in rural South Alabama. He passed all the entrance exams except the physical which I always felt he deliberately failed so his actual acceptance would be denied. He was, without doubt, the most gregarious person I have ever known and did not want to leave his friends. They wanted to go to college together and continue the good times they all enjoyed.

Those of us who had the privilege of becoming young adults in the sixties were truly blessed. We got to live in the very best of times. Love was free and so were we—free from the worries of today's world. Alcohol and a little marijuana were the worst things about which we had to make decisions. Those were the days when locks were on cars and houses but used infrequently. Partying quite often resulted in a very serious hangover but that dissipated within a few hours. There were a few students from very wealthy families but most of us were from very similar middle class families and this equality gave us very large circles of friends.

I was the studious, dedicated co-ed who made good grades as demanded by my scholarship. I tutored several football players and wrote their term papers. Those services paid me very well. I commuted to campus and continued to live at home with my parents and was therefore regarded as prudish. I had nothing to hide from my parents and was happy to continue living at home. In these days, I'm sure many people will find it difficult to believe that I maintained my virginity until Allen and I were married when I was almost twenty-one. I am thankful that my parents instilled some puritanical values in me. The value system of most young people from then until now is a zillion miles apart.

Allen loved the party life and never outgrew his need for constant socializing. We were married November 27, 1965, in a very small, private ceremony. He and I were fortunate enough to get good paying jobs and had a very good marriage for several years. In his free time, he enjoyed hunting and fishing and became more and more involved in his hobbies as our income allowed. He became well known in regional and some national circles as being an exceptional hunter and fisherman.

I had, over the years, become very career oriented and opened my own sub-contracting firm. Professional recognition and monetary reward became extremely important to me, so much so that my workaholism was in full flourish. I traveled extensively and so did he—he to sporting events and I to work. We were, for many months, like ships passing in the night. I never gave a thought to the fact that my husband needed more from me than I was giving.

After I had my hysterectomy at the age of 28, I knew that children were never going to be a part of my life. So I filled it with work, arts and crafts, cooking, and friends. My nest was never full so I did not have to experience that empty nest syndrome of many of my friends. My life has been very full and I have no regrets that I am childless. Not all women have to be mothers. There are many other worthwhile roles that need filling.

Our marriage was a very good one for several years. We never had a fuss or cross words. We simply grew to distance. When I returned home from a business trip to the west coast, my maid happened to be cleaning the house that day. She came to me with tears in her eyes and said she needed to talk with me. As we sat down she pulled something out of her smock pocket that she had found in my bed that did not belong to me. It was evident that something was wrong in my house. Allen was out of state on a hunting trip and when he returned home, he found my note telling him that he needed to talk to my attorney. I moved only my clothes and personal items and left everything else for him. Our line of communication was completely severed and I was unwilling to forgive his actions of infidelity. I accept most of the fault for the failure of my first marriage but the shock of his violation of my trust took a long time to overcome. All of that now seems more like a dream than reality and I rarely give any thought to that long ago relationship. Things that are too painful to remember, we truly tend to forget.

Allen remarried sixty-three days after our divorce was final and he died a couple of years later of lung cancer.

# RESPONSIBILITY TO OURSELVES

Living a good life is a personal choice. One of the first lessons my father taught me was *if you play, be prepared to pay*. Once I had a clear understanding of the relationship between cause and effect, I knew that if I wanted something, I had to do all the necessary things to get it. This one principle allows me to plan for the future.

Unfortunately, our culture teaches the opposite of responsibility. If something good happens, it's luck. If something bad happens, it's someone else's fault. This belief sabotages all the power that can be found in taking responsibility for our lives.

We are always responsible for our attitudes. When I was a child and would tell my mother that someone made me *mad*, Mother would always remind me that *I made me mad*. Whatever someone else had done was their responsibility, not mine. Even in really detestable situations, we still have the power to control our attitudes and actions. If we are caught in traffic, we can yell and curse, honk our horn or rail against the highway engineers. Or we can listen to music, have a conversation, or watch others react. But, either way, we are still stuck in traffic.

We each have the power of choices in our lives, yet we so often and so easily give it up. Seizing control of our choices is one powerful way to take responsibility for our lives. Because we have the power of choice, we have control over the actions we choose to take.

Many times we do not have complete control over the consequences. Once a cause is set into motion, it can be difficult or sometimes, impossible to stop. But we are still responsible for those consequences and we know that we are mature individuals when we accept responsibility for our attitude, choices and actions.

I have learned through my personal challenges that the only way we can move through adversity is to maintain a strong, positive mental attitude. A positive attitude is strong enough to take us through challenging situations and will consistently lead us to the correct answers and solutions.

Adversity is not negative. When we overcome an adverse situation we gain both strength and character. It forces us to stay on top of circumstances because it reminds us that we are stronger than we could ever imagine. It is a mindset that actually helps us to flip a situation upside down. Adversity and challenges simply show us a better way to achieve our goals and dreams. I've heard it said that *tough times never last, but tough people do.* Relax and be positive, no matter what! Each layer of my life has helped me to have a deeper understanding of these principles and each experience has strengthened my determination and creativity.

Our life is God's gift to us but what we do with our life is our gift to God. To be truly happy in life, we must learn to allow ourselves to do what makes our heart sing.

When someone shows you who they really are, believe them the first time. If a friend betrays your trust, know that they will do it again if given the opportunity. My deepest hurts have given me my greatest life messages. If you can learn from my mistakes you will know that the worst of times usually become the best of times when you go forward with hope and faith. My being totally honest with you and your being totally honest with yourself can help you to help yourself.

We all have the capability to control our own happiness. Our attitudes, more than experiences, are within our control. Learning to eliminate or at least manage negativity goes far in creating optimism. My husband and I have pledged to ourselves to allow zero negativity in our home. On more than one occasion, we have shown visitors to the door who were spewing negativism. When we find peace in our own homes, we are at our happiest. Cooperation with each other rather than competition is also key to that happiness.

Laughter, that deep belly laugh, uncontrollable giggling or just a tiny smile maker is good for the soul. My husband is such a joyful person and he makes me laugh daily. Recently, someone asked me what I would miss most about Gene and without giving it any thought, I answered *laughter*. My happiness quotient has grown exponentially since we married.

Being grateful will rachet up that that happiness quotient as well. Writing thank you notes to friends and family members brighten the day of the composer but much more importantly, that of the recipient. These notes require so little of us but mean so much to others.

Finding a job we love is such a gift to us and to the world. Whatever we enjoy doing, we will do well. Since I am an over-achiever by my nature, I enjoy doing productive things. Meaningful goals with tangible results satisfy me and make me happy.

Kindness to others will boost our mood. The happiness we feel is in direct proportion to the love and goodness we share.

Happiness is ever elusive but relief from unhappiness is attainable. Whatever someone did to you in the past has no power over you in the present. Happiness is not another place but *this place*; not another hour but *this hour*.

Being true to yourself and your needs is not being selfish. If you cheat yourself, then you are not whole and you cheat everyone in your life.

When I discovered or finally admitted that fear had been driving my decisions, I found that it was actually due to a disconnect between who I thought I should be and who I really was. My authentic self is the one who flourishes unselfconsciously during the happiest, most fulfilled times in my life.

When beauty and vigor diminish, it should not affect our sense of worth or identity in any way. As a matter of fact, as the body begins to weaken, the light of consciousness and creativity can shine more brightly. The goodness within us will emerge more easily.

# THE SIGNS WERE THERE

Rex had been my banker for thirteen years and we had a wonderful professional, platonic relationship. Most of his customers would have told you that he was the very best banker in his organization. When I borrowed money from that institution, through Rex, I would never have considered being late with re-payment. All of us felt that we were re-paying *him* and could never let him down. That was the consensus of opinion of his clients. He went out of his way to help me in every way financially. As long as I kept him abreast of my needs, he handled them and for that I'll be forever grateful.

When Rex learned that I had divorced my first husband, he immediately asked me for a date. I jokingly, and at the same time, seriously said that I was sure he asked all his single clients out. I thanked him but graciously declined; explaining that I needed a good banker much more than I needed a boyfriend. He never took NO for an answer. He called me every few days, on the pretense of just checking on me or to ask my opinion on something insignificant—any excuse for contact. After several months of this, I decided to let him escort me to a Christmas party of my civic club. Knowing that he knew most of the predominantly male members would leave me free to do my duties for the event without his being left alone or uncomfortable. I had little time to spend with him during that evening and felt that he would not enjoy himself enough to ask me out again. I could not have been more wrong! I received beautiful roses the next day and several phone calls from him.

I did agree to go out to dinner and dancing the following weekend. Montgomery was small enough that I never went out without seeing a few to several people I knew well and knew that we would be in one of those group situations most of the evening. I had been going to theater events and out to dinner with a couple of guys since my divorce and one of them just happened to be where we went to dance. Montgomery was also small enough that everyone knew everyone else's business and someone remarked to Rex that one of the guys and I had been dating.

When Bob went to the men's room, Rex left our table and went to the men's room as well. I never gave it a thought until the next day when Bob called to tell me he had been threatened, both personally and professionally by Rex and that he was told never to call or see me again. And this was after the second date! I should have seen the sign then but was so naïve that I rationalized that Rex was simply taking care of me. Bob was a bit rough around the edges but in general, a very good man who had done well in his construction business.

Rex continued to try to consume my every free minute after work and on weekends. Within the first month of our going out in the evenings, he wanted me to meet his daughters and I wanted that opportunity. After about six weeks he was transferred to another area of the state, about a 4 hour drive from Montgomery and I welcomed that distance. I was sure he would quickly become involved with someone there and my life would become mine again. We had been friends for so long that I was happy to help him pack his household goods to move to his new job. I also went down for a weekend to set up his kitchen, hang some pictures and make his new apartment livable. I knew that his new job would be very demanding and require long hours and weekends at the office. Or so I thought! Every Friday afternoon, as soon as he could leave the bank, he would drive to Montgomery and stay until very early Monday morning, getting up at 2 or 3 am to dress and return straight to the office. And then, the same schedule, week after week. I received several calls from him daily and considered this to be thoughtful concern. It felt really good to have someone care so much! He called enough that he had a play by play insight into my work and personal activities—after all, he was my banker and gave me guidance and I was most appreciative.

Rex knew all the right ways to impress and impress me he did. Gifts, flowers, cards, trips, special events—all were mine without even asking. He seemed to spend every minute trying to please me or make me happy. I was truly courted as though I were a princess. I was included any time he had business trips out of town or out of state. He loved to call on Thursday and have me meet him in Atlanta or New York or wherever for a weekend retreat. While there he would treat me to spas, shopping, fancy dinners, theater, sightseeing—anything to please me.

If we were in Montgomery for the weekend, one or both of his girls would usually be with us and I truly enjoyed getting to know them and do a bit of *smothering*. His girls appeared to be very pleased with some *sanity* in their lives. In those early days, Rex really was very good to both of them.

He invited me to go on a cruise and since this was my first cruise experience, I was very excited about it. As I was leaving Montgomery to drive to his place, I went by his pharmacy to pick up some prescription refills he had ordered. Until that time, I did not realize how many medications he was taking nor that he was taking some for depression. My sheer stupidity made me think I could fix his depression because I did not realize until much later what a very serious mental illness depression is. I could never have dreamed the depths of his particular disorder and it took me many years to grasp how consuming the illness can be. It consumes not only the sufferer of depression but all of those whose lives they touch.

During the cruise and while being together 24/7 I began to see some signs I should have heeded but did not. One day he sent me to the on-board spa for the *works*. After a full day of pampering I felt wonderfully rested and ready for a night of entertainment. Our ship was in port for the evening so after dinner we decided to go for a walk and see how the natives lived. Many others from our ship did the same and we wound up at a nice nightclub which had a great band. After a few dances, one of the very nice gentlemen on our ship asked me to dance and before our dance had really begun, Rex broke in. My new dance partner and I were both shocked. Several dances later, he asked again if I'd dance with him. I was getting up to join him on the floor when Rex lost it and went into a complete yelling, cursing rage at that man. Needless to say, embarrassment was the least of my reactions. I was furious with Rex and demanded that we return to the ship. On our return walk, he reverted to the sweet, considerate, attentive Rex I was accustomed to and began telling me how much he loved me and wanted me to marry him. He cast aspersions toward the gentleman who had showed me a tiny bit of attention and said some very unfavorable things about him, none of which I had noticed. Such as how he held me on the dance floor, had been watching me all evening—just that he had a very bad feeling about him overall. By the time we returned to our suite, I had calmed down and had been convinced that my protector was doing his job. We did not see that other gentleman again while on the cruise, thank goodness.

When we got back to the ship, Rex gave me a gorgeous wool cape he had purchased for me while I was being treated at the spa. He had shopped all day and bought nice gifts for his girls, his mother and my parents.

The next morning as we started to breakfast, he was extremely quiet and distant and seemed preoccupied. I decided to go back to the suite and read and nap. This would be our last day on the ship and we would be returning to Miami overnight and would then drive back to Alabama.

I had known for a while that Rex was stressed at work. As president of a bank with many problems, he had his work cut out for him. He was an individual who always thought his way was the only way to solve problems. Trying to satisfy a board of directors comprised of businessmen from the local community and, at the same time, satisfy the demands of the holding company put additional stress on the existing situations. His inability to compromise created an untenable environment for Rex and he was put on leave for six months.

We had been married only nine months when we found ourselves with two girls in college, his mother who had Alzheimer's disease to support, and a house to sell while the interest rate was in the teens. Fortunately, we were able to sell the house I had redecorated as soon as we put it on the market. We bought a well-used mobile home and parked it on my parents' farm property. Relocating to be near our parents was a blessing and I have never regretted that but the circumstances under which we relocated were anything but desirable. Rex had to give up his company car when he was dismissed from the bank and we became a one-car family, living in a mobile home in the country, our belongings in storage and a very indefinite future. For the entire time we had been married, as I look back on it, my life had been total chaos. Three moves in less than a year were equal to all the moves I had had in my previous life of thirty-five years. For the first time in my life I felt that I was living in a deprived way and I was. The expenses of supporting two apartments in a university town (his girls refused to room together) as well as other educational expenses and taking care of his mom left little to play with. Rex was exhibiting such depressive behavior, I knew I had to help him through this and I had married him for better or worse. During this six month hiatus I gave up almost all contact with my family and friends and concentrated only on Rex. His ups and downs kept me on such a yo-yo that I never knew on which side of the bed he would wake. I began to see the disease of depression as it truly was. There were times when Rex would go to bed for days on end and I would wait on him completely—meals in bed, medications dispensed on schedule and I simply waited for him to call on me. This was such a different way of living for me that my entire system had to be in shock.

Finally, almost six months after losing his job at the bank, he was re-hired by the real estate division of that same holding company, with benefits and same salary restored. This gave me a tremendous sense of relief and I felt that our lives would quickly return to *normal*. He would be working from the home office in Montgomery so I spent almost three months looking at houses in the city. No matter what I found that

I thought had potential—whether a fixer-upper or a newly constructed house or anything in between, he tore it apart. Nothing pleased him. So he decided he'd commute to Montgomery and we would build a house in the country.

He was back in his element and among his old friends and customers. He, once again, on a daily basis, was enjoying two-martini luncheons and stopping by to have drinks and socialize in the afternoon. I was living in the country, without a car and isolated from everyone except my parents. When my friends called I made excuses not to see them and so, some of them, after a while, stopped calling. I spent my days working in the yard, growing a vegetable garden, crocheting and entertaining myself however I could. I was no more than his maid servant and actually was willing to accept this role for the short term.

I was the obedient wife and handed over all power to my husband. He was the master manipulator and knew exactly how to make me feel sorry for him. I felt that being his queen and having him as my king was my role in life.

Two or three nights a week he arrived home at nine or ten o'clock and assured me his after hour meetings were business. The other night or two of the week he would come home, go right to bed and have his dinner served in bed. After all, he needed his rest.

After about a year of this, I felt he had time to adjust to the new job and started talking about building the house. I had been working on the plans and was ready to find a builder. But, as I look back, he had me exactly where he wanted me—barefoot and isolated, so to speak. He came up with every excuse in the world to delay the beginning of construction. I finally demanded that he buy me a car and for my birthday, I got a used, late model car. This was fine with me as long as it provided reliable transportation.

Starting the house would be after many months of interviewing contractors and sub-contractors. I learned that when an individual is totally miserable in his own skin that no one human can please him. I finally hired the contractor myself. After the French drain and slab were completed and our contractor, Buddy Russell and his crew worked for one day, Rex came home and prepared a 10 point punch list—after only one day of actual construction. He was out of the house early the next morning to drive to Montgomery to work and left that stupid list for me to give to Buddy Russell. I apologetically handed it to Buddy when he arrived to begin his day of work. He looked at the list, said nothing for a few minutes but when he did speak, he spoke volumes.

"If Mr. Smith is going to stay awake nights worrying about what I'm doing, he doesn't need me. Mrs. Smith, tell your husband to take care of the banking and I'll take care of the building," he said.

That night, when Rex got home, I delivered Buddy's message verbatim and Rex was smart enough to understand the full impact of that message. From that day forward, he had high regard for our wonderful builder who did an excellent job for us.

After about six months of construction, Rex went into the deepest depression I'd ever seen. He took a month off work and basically stayed in bed. Continuing to coordinate the construction project and taking care of him was almost more than I could handle. His mood swings were very extreme and he took copious amounts of anti-depressants. And then, added to all of that, he drank excessive amounts of alcohol and there was no reasoning with him when he was under those influences. Now that he had pulled me into his web and isolated me from almost everyone else, I began to have some very bizarre health problems. My hypertension was very difficult to control, yet I continued to assure my doctors that I had very little stress! Really! Fibrositis became the bane of my existence and I was very sick with high fevers, pain, all over body aches and inflammation. Rex seemed to be much better and took great pride in taking care of me—the almost invalid wife. Shopping, traveling and most other normal activities were too much for me. He was happiest when I was under his control. He saw that I had all the domestic help and caregivers I needed. When I was diagnosed with a pheochromacytoma, a rare adrenal mass, he delighted in being the poor Rex with the sick wife. My recovery was slow but it really did take my hitting the bottom—by this I simply mean that I was very ill physically, mentally, and emotionally—before I took my life in my hands again and determined that I was worth saving. As my recovery began and I started searching for answers to what had really happened to me, I realized that Rex's toxicity had been almost fatal for me.

By reading every self-help book I could find, getting off prescription medications and taking alternative herbs and vitamins, I slowly began to regain my health. From time to time, as long as Rex and I were married, he would actually say that he liked it much better when I was sick. I was determined to arrive on the other side of the deep abyss in which I found myself, a stronger person in every way—physically, mentally, emotionally and most of all, spiritually. After all, by allowing him to control me as I had, God had been my only ally on many occasions. I must admit that Rex Smith taught me more accidentally than I have learned deliberately in a lifetime. He showed me what the faces of pure evil and hatred look like. He was smart enough or more succinctly—I was stupid enough to allow his total control of me and everything in my life. I now know my weaknesses but I certainly recognize how strong I really am. He taught me that a sick mind is a very dangerous thing and should be avoided at all costs. He taught me that money is truly the root of much evil and to worship it is a poor excuse for a supreme being. I learned that friends are more precious than any jewels on this earth. He taught me that no man can stand alone, even if he thinks he can. He helped me to see the true value of good relationships by his complete disregard for all other human beings, even those who tried to love him. I learned that being my self is fine in all circles. I do not have to impress anyone, anywhere, anytime. I'm fine just as I am. He taught me that love does not have a monetary value and cannot be bought. I learned from him and by his example, that an individual can fool some of the people some of the time but not all of the people, all of the time. I learned from him that trust, once lost, can never be regained. He also showed me that when someone shows their true self, see them for who they really are. I learned from him that "so called love" is tense, competitive, angst-filled, questioning, and downright uncomfortable.

When Rex would say that he liked it better when I was sick, I now know that what he was really saying was that he liked it better when I was weak and in his control. I can tell the world that I had to get a divorce to get better! There are other people in this world that can learn from my example.

Getting a divorce from Rex should have been the end of his trying to control me but it was not. If anything, he stepped up his efforts because he was not used to the type of resistance I exhibited. He did everything in his power to control me financially and only by the grace of God and the fairness of our justice system did I escape losing everything. I left him on a Friday afternoon, under escort of the sheriff's department and by Monday at noon, all credit cards and bank accounts were closed and/or cancelled. He felt that he could still control me by controlling my access to money. But he did not realize that I would have lived on the streets before I would have gone back to him. He was so certain I would return to him that for the first six months or so after I left our house, he told everyone I was on a trip! And was I ever on a trip!

I was stalked, followed, photographed, had my apartment invaded by strangers, and finally had men attempt to break into my home while brandishing guns. These actions show how extreme his attempts were to control me but he failed miserably. I had finally gained enough inner strength and faith in God that I could resist his persistent evil and efforts.

During the divorce proceedings, he actually forced my attorney's car off the road. He had followed him from the courthouse after a hearing and when my attorney realized what was happening, he tried to lose him by going into a store where he pretended to shop. Rex was brazen enough to wait in the parking lot for him to return to his car and then resume his following. After he forced him off the road, he honked the horn and was sure my attorney recognized him as he went by.

I married Rex for all the wrong reasons—he had two daughters who I thought would become the daughters I never had. He was president of the bank and I liked the social status that position provided. I enjoyed the prestige, the travel, and all the perks that were part of our lives. And the Rex Smith he had shown me most of the time was caring, generous, affectionate but a bit prone to moodiness and quick temper. I had not heeded the signs I had seen and can now admit that I was in total denial. I did not know myself at that time so there was no way for me to truly know someone else. The pedestal on which I had been placed prior to our marriage would soon be knocked from under me.

Had I known then what I know now, I would never have married him. But, as is so often the case, hindsight is truly 20/20.

As soon as we were married, I became the official link to the bank account between Rex and his girls. I would get phone calls from them requesting funds and I would justify and rationalize these expenditures to Rex. When our means were reduced, after his dismissal from the bank, we should have all worked together to reduce their expenditures but that did not happen.

Rex would never handle things in a civil tone but had to get into yelling matches with his daughters and always ended up casting aspersions toward their biological mother. There would be long spells of no contact from either daughter and then, when they would call me, I would try to make things right between them and their father. This was accomplished many times during the twenty years we were together but Rex would invariably get into a drunken stupor, call one of them and this relationship dysfunction would repeat its harm. I would try to soothe all of them; Rex included, and did so many, many times.

But, there finally was a *straw that broke the camel's back.* His youngest daughter was getting married to a wonderful young man from Ohio. They had been living there for a few years and most of their friends were there.

It was logical for them to be married where they lived, so we had the wedding in Ohio. She wanted me to make their wedding and groom's cakes and I was delighted to do so. She also asked that I come up early enough to help her put together a lovely reception for about 250 people. Old friends, college classmates, and family came from all over the country and it was to be a grand event. Rex promised her, and me, that he would behave and be very civil to her mother.

Everything was fine until he began drinking about noon on the wedding day. By the six o'clock ceremony, he was well into his cups and when asked by the pastor,

"Who giveth this woman?"

Rex responded in his loudest, most despicable voice,

"Her stepmother, Bonnie, and I do, and that other woman!"

I have never been so embarrassed or hurt in my life. At that very moment, I realized that I could no longer trust him, in any way, and knew that I would leave him. He had, after all, promised *me* that he would behave himself. He had made me believe that he would honor his daughter's wedding day enough to be civil to his ex-wife. But, by this time in our marriage, everything was about *him*. His bottle and he were almost constant companions and the prescription drug consumption was escalating also. By this time, I realized that he was actually completely unaware of his conversations and actions while very under the influence. But this was not one of those times. He was drunk but not that drunk. Her wedding from that moment forward was completely ruined. We all went through the motions, carriage rides, receiving line, toasts and reception but the tension was so thick it could have been cut along with the wedding cake. I finally got him to leave the reception about ten o'clock and we went back to our hotel.

The young bride and groom came by our hotel the next morning, fully expecting a genuine apology from Rex but he began a tirade regarding her mother. His daughter stood up to him, expressing her total disappointment, distrust, and disrespect and asked him to get help for his drinking and drug addictions. As always, he denied having problems and at that point, she severed her relationship with her father and has maintained that separation as far as I know. She has done this rightfully so! I feel certain that her life has been much more stable and level without him than it could ever be with him in it.

My life with Rex, from that day forward was tenuous. I truly believe that trust is a very large part of love and that one cannot exist without the other. He never acknowledged, even to me, that he was at fault.

One thing that I do not understand even now is that when Rex and I were alone, he would usually, until very close to the end of our living together, revert to the affectionate, kind, caring person. It was usually, only when other people were with us, that the rude, hateful Rex would show off. When talking to other women who are or were married to *controllers*, their public personalities are usually acceptable but those shown behind closed doors are the ones to be feared. The only way I can explain his behavior reversal is that he was attempting to show the world that I was his personal property and he could treat me any way he pleased. He also knew that I was polite enough and concerned enough with others' comforts that I would not create a public scene.

Realizing that I was property and valued only as such is very demeaning. It took me several years to develop my core value and to discover my true self. I pledged to myself to do just that before I would become involved in another marital relationship. I had to accomplish this before there would be enough of me to share with another spouse.

For the many women and/or men who live or have lived with controllers, I hope for you to find balance in your relationships. Competition in various areas of your relationships will feed that unhealthy union. If effort is made to complement each other in every area of your life, your closeness and value to each other will grow exponentially. That constant tension and dis-ease will be erased forever. True love, comfort and happiness can be yours.

# GUILT VS. GRIEF

Guilt is deserved when parents abuse their children or when they put their own lives before the needs of their children. When parents become emotionally unavailable to their children, guilt should be experienced. When spouses cheat, whether found out or not, guilt has to be experienced.

Grief, on the other hand, is of true regret, when there is sadness or loss of a loved one. It is possible to work through the various stages of grief and to completely recover from it. Guilt, however, is a permanent malady unless one is willing to ask forgiveness and to amend whatever wrong has been done. Sometimes though, this is not possible. If a spouse dies before differences are resolved, it is too late. Living each day as though it could be our last is the best resolution to guilt.

We are responsible for our actions and attitudes but if we have children who refuse to stop wasting intellectual and creative potential, we cannot take the credit for their self-destructiveness. Nor can we take the credit if they have become great successes.

We must determine if we are part of their problem or part of their solution. Sometimes, we must give up our efforts to make things different. Sometimes, even when *giving up* makes us feel hopeless, it is the right thing to do.

There are influences and experiences that have nothing to do with us or with what we tried to teach them or help them understand. Sometimes withdrawing completely from their lives is the only way they learn to appreciate us and our efforts.

By dropping all excuses and putting our hopes and talents on the line, we can open a promising future. Our lives are not small and should not be regarded as such. Our lives are large when we are true to ourselves despite fear, fatigue, and doubt and we can serve the world in more ways than imaginable. In fact, we just might save the world or at least one person. When we actually see the world through the eyes of another, it is a type of rebirth and sometimes we and that other individual are both reborn. We must know that no matter how much at fault the other person is, we can't fix him. We can, however, change ourselves and hope that he will change by our example.

My husband and I have such utter peace and calm in our lives and wish to share that with others. We try to avoid situations and/or people who seem filled with chaos and confusion. All of that can even be transmitted by telephone. That negative energy, given the right environment can multiply just as positive energy does.

I am a firm believer in that if we do not condemn behaviors, we condone them. If each of us lives our life seeking peace and harmony, surely the world will be a better place because of our presence.

# LAST TRIP TOGETHER

Rex had been in a very deep depression, probably the deepest I had ever seen, for several weeks. But as was always the case, he could go from being in bed with covers pulled up over his head to singing in the shower in a fifteen minute time span. When he came out of the shower, he announced that I needed a vacation and I did. I needed a vacation from his mental illness. I agreed to go visit his oldest daughter and her family in Colorado Springs.

Rex insisted on making our flight reservations but booked us for only one way. I usually handled all travel details and always made return reservations. He told me he would book our trip home when we arrived at the Denver airport. Since he was drinking excessively and his paranoia was in full swing, I dared not push that issue. He decided that someone would surely steal all his guns and ammo while we were away (none of our other possessions had any importance!) so he loaded the trunk with pistols, rifles, AK47's, etc. and called a friend in Montgomery who agreed to keep them until we got back.

I had had an ureteroscopy a week earlier and still had the stent in which was to be removed in a few days. As always, Rex thought only of himself and decided we'd get my stent removed on the way to the airport. We arrived at the doctor's office about 4:45 pm and my stent was out by 5:00 pm. The doctor and Rex were drinking buddies of long standing and so we were in for a marathon. When we left the doctor's office, we dropped the guns off at our friend's house. They begged me not to go on to Birmingham with him. The good Lord does take care of drunks and fools—Rex being the drunk and my being the fool! I did, however, know that this would be my last trip with Rex. We checked into the motel about midnight only to have to be at the airport by 4:00 am. I was so uncomfortable and was bleeding profusely after having the stent removed that I never even fell asleep that night. Rex ordered a bloody Mary as soon as we were in the air and continued his drinking binge all the way to Denver.

As soon as we retrieved our luggage, we started to the counter to book our return flight. He was ahead of me since I was walking more slowly than usual. I heard raised voices and looked ahead to see him creating a commotion. There were four people in line at that window and he was demanding that another window be opened just for him. As soon as the attendant recognized his drunken state, she closed the window and walked away. I was far enough away to be able to pretend I didn't know him but close enough to hear some of the remarks. When four uniformed security guards approached him, I turned to walk away. But, by this time, he realized he probably needed me and was calling to me. I should have kept walking in the opposite direction and boarded the next flight back to Birmingham. I regretted not having done just that many times over the next three weeks. After I assured the security guards that I would handle him and that I would drive the rental car to his daughter's, they agreed to let him go. We did not book the return flight until much later.

Rex had sobered up a bit by the time we arrived at his daughter's in the early evening. We visited briefly, ate a bite of dinner and were off to bed.

His daughter and her husband had finally gotten into their new house and there were many loose ends needing attention. We had given them the lot on which the house had been constructed. We had also equipped their kitchen with top of the line appliances. She had become a very good cook and we encouraged her to pursue that endeavor. Rex decided we would have their yard landscaped while we were there. We hired laborers and with their help, planted shrubs and trees and sodded their lawn. After several days of very hard work, Rex decided we would go to Crested Butte for a few days. When we left Alabama, our return trip was open ended.

When we left his daughter's, we simply told her we'd come back there before returning home to Alabama—still very open ended. As soon as we were on the road, Rex became his most loving, affectionate, debonair self and pampered me constantly—breakfast in bed, spa treatments, roses, champagne, shopping, sightseeing—you name it and it was mine! I should have known that this bubble would soon burst. I decided to take a day to myself, stay in bed, rest, read a good book and give my body some healing time from my recent kidney procedure. Our suite was very comfortable with two king sized beds—his and mine. He decided to go sightseeing for part of the day so I could have peace and quiet. How very considerate of him! When he came back mid-afternoon, it was obvious he had done a lot of walking/hiking as he was very dusty and had perspired enough that his shirt was watermarked. He announced that he had found a very beautiful place that I must see. Rex was up bright and early the next morning, ready to go. We had a leisurely breakfast and he picked up a picnic basket from the deli next door. We drove through the aspen and fern forests and saw lots of grazing cows but few other cars or people. He drove, making many turns onto smaller and smaller highways and graveled roads until we finally arrived at a very beautiful lake. A huge log had been felled near the water's edge and made a very comfortable seat. Rex served me a nice glass of my favorite wine and a delicious roast beef sandwich with all the trimmings. Then came the most delicious strawberry cheesecake I've ever eaten. This was one of the most gorgeous, serene places I had ever seen. I was savoring the fine lunch as well as the scenery when Rex came over to massage my upper back and neck. Almost immediately his hands went to my throat and he began to choke me. I finally realized what was really happening. As I write this, my breath is very short—just the memory of that moment is truly breathtaking! Somehow, I put my hands on his wrists and began to push upward. He continued to tighten his grip and I continued to push. As I began to black out, he quickly released his grip, turned away, and I could hear the crunch of small pebbles under his feet as he walked to the car. While I was recovering my breath and my senses, I was sure he was going to drive away and leave me for the bears and wolves to devour. The car did not start and I finally regained my strength enough to stand. When I turned around to face him, he was in the passenger's seat, knees pulled up in the fetal position and sobbing audibly.

I have never needed to see another human being as much as I did at that moment! I knew that I had to drive us out of there. Since I can get lost in a phone booth, I had no idea where to turn but as so often happens in my life, God had to be on my shoulder. Somehow I got us back to Crested Butte! Not a word was spoken by either of us on the drive back to our motel. When we arrived there, we got out of the car and went to our room.

All of us have seen small children come out of wet clothing. And, they always wind up as hard rolls of fabric. Rex's clothes were rolled in a ball on the floor beside his bed. He climbed into bed, pulled the covers up over his head and for the next two days got up only to go to the bathroom. No food. No bath. Nothing to drink. No medication—at least not in my presence. I would go out for meals and return to my bed to read. I slept with *one eye open*. I am still amazed that I had the internal fortitude and patience to wait him out. After two days of sulking, he got up, took a shower and appeared to be himself again. We have never discussed or even mentioned the events of Lost Lake. He was by now ready to return to his daughter's. We went back there for three days and by all appearances, everything seemed *normal*. When we left there, I assumed we would be going straight to the airport to return to Alabama. He announced that we were going to look for real estate in Colorado. He had the grandiose idea that we would buy some acreage and build a house there. And that we would not even return home—just stay in Colorado and build the house. He had it all planned that the movers could pack our belongings from the house in Alabama and bring it to us. I knew that after a few days, he would be in another mood, but only God could know which way or when that wind would blow. I remained as calm as I could and simply bided my time until I would return home. In hindsight, I now know that I was so numbed by the years of being controlled by his whims and moods that I was powerless to pull away from that control. His ultimate goal was to isolate me from all family, friends, and all things with which I was familiar and comfortable. There are, I am certain, many other woman who are trapped in relationships which are just as dysfunctional as mine was. The one thing that would have further complicated my situation would have been having children. I now know why God did not give me any.

I do not know if I could have managed another obstacle in my life. My personal survival was in question many times. His denying fault and blaming others made me question my sanity constantly.

The how and why of his deep seated anger has always fascinated me. Having lost his father at the tender age of 9 had to have been the beginning of his frustrations. He recounted many times that he became *man of the house* at the time of his father's death. His irrationality was hidden from almost everyone who knew him. The B. Rex Smith with whom I lived for 20+ years has finally surfaced and most find it impossible to comprehend this complex human being. On the one hand, he was the adoring, charismatic, debonair gentleman any woman would be glad to call husband. One the other hand, he was the difficult, sadistic, hateful, spiteful, demon-possessed human being. I have heard him curse God when it would or would not rain at our farm. He would stand on the deck and swear at God if it was lightning.

And then, he could mimic what he thought others wanted of him. But in the end, he always took from others whatever he wanted. The true miracle of Rex's life is that, with little formal higher education, be became a fine banker who enjoyed a stellar reputation for a long time.

After he began taking Prozac, he became extremely narcissistic. He would primp like a teenage girl readying for her first date, sometimes taking as much as two hours to bathe and dress. He would walk outside with no clothes on. If someone happened to come down our driveway at one of those times, he made no effort to cover himself. No one's time meant anything—only his time had value.

This last trip was just what I needed to make me know that my marriage was over in every way except legally. And that is a very long and detailed chapter in my life. The three and a half years of fighting for that final divorce decree was certainly draining—physically, mentally and financially. More. Later.

By the time this trip was over, I promised myself that I wouldn't be bound by the belief that I'm supposed to stay in anything—whether it's a relationship, a job, a house, or a circumstance—if it makes me miserable. I found the courage to find my own happiness. My experience taught me that life without enjoyment and peace of mind is not living. I owe it to myself to live beautifully, and I do!

# MEXICO! OH MEXICO!

Rex and I had been living in the same house but with great tension for several months. I finally asked him to enter a drug treatment program and assured him that I would walk with him through every step. By this time, I had admitted to myself that I would get out of our marriage but was willing to sacrifice my happiness if I could help him recover from his addictions to prescription drugs and alcohol. When I mentioned rehab, he became completely enraged and assured me that he did not have a problem. I simply told him that he had choices to make—treatment for his problems or divorce. This was my attempt at intervention but I believe that once the *divorce* word is spoken that the relationship is altered forever. Trust and commitment are diminished beyond repair. He decided to go on a trip rather than seek help. I welcomed his departure and volunteered to pack for him. Since he couldn't or wouldn't tell me where he was going or for how long, I wanted to be sure he'd have everything he needed. And needless to say, he was prepared for a very long journey by the time I closed the fourth suitcase! He would be prepared for any event—from swim trunks to casual to his finest suits. After having spent all day getting him ready to go, I thought he would never leave. About 11:00 pm I heard him slam the back door, start his car and leave. I think I took my first deep breath (or sigh of relief) in days. I went upstairs and found this note on the kitchen counter:

August 20, 1996

Bonnie:

No goodbyes, ok; and thanks for the memories—most of all the good ones. Just want you to be happy.

When you talk to Sally, tell her that I will be ok, and that I love her, and that she can get relief for her depression as early as possible. My love also to granddaughter Cathy and John.

Please care for Bobo and Lazy Dee—they are good dogs!

Don't get over friendly with Mitchell, ok. Not trustworthy—and double check everything he does. Money loans—up to you—always sob stories! Tell Mitchell to feed and water cripple chick also or put her to sleep. Call Cattle Company when grass begins to thin out and sell the steers—sometime in September.

Get the roofing you want. Also, there are some good designs on asphalt shingles. Total coverage about 36 squares. Labor cost should be in the $25 to $30 a square, on top of original shingles. Plenty of framing support to hold old and new shingles.

Take care and hope your health continues to improve. Hope we can be friends again someday.

Rex"

I did not feel safe enough to go to bed that night so I busied myself with mundane chores. Several of my friends knew that the tension between us was great and were keeping very close tabs on me. Thank God! I needed all the support I could get at one of the lowest points of my life. I had planned to grow old with Rex. We had been through much and made great sacrifices to take care of his mother, to educate his two daughters and to help take care of my father until his death and then to continue to assist my mother in every way possible. We had no choice but to accept those responsibilities. I've seen that in most families, no matter how many children there are, that one steps up to the plate. Rex was the one in his family and I was the one in mine.

During the afternoon of Rex's first day of missing in action, my friend Carter Sanders came over to check on me. Carter is an angel in disguise to many people—his mother, my friend Nadine and certainly to me. He is a friend who can be counted on when one is most needed. I will be forever grateful to him for spending that night on my sofa, on guard, in the event Rex decided to return to harm me.

Rex's oldest daughter called from Colorado Springs and could tell from my voice that something was askew. I had no choice but to tell her that her father had gone to an undisclosed location and when she asked specifically if he had a gun with him, I had to tell her that he had a pistol. We both felt that he probably was suicidal and God only knew what he would do—to himself and/or to others. There is an inherited gene in Rex's family for depression and several of his uncles had had problems. Because she was so concerned about his state of mind she called the local sheriff's office and asked them to issue an alert to locate her father. When the sheriff called me to see what was really going on, I assured him that Rex had gone on his own on an obviously well planned trip. Since the sheriff had been a friend of my parents for years he knew that my judgment of the situation was fairly close to fact. When he asked me where I thought he had gone, I guessed Mexico but why I chose that location is still a mystery to me.

At the time of Rex's departure, we were having the interior of the house repainted. I proceeded with that and also had a new roof installed. He told me before he left he would continue to have his social security and retirement checks deposited into our joint checking account which usually carried a sizeable balance. Since day one of our marriage I had issued almost all of our household checks and made whatever decisions were needed regarding the household. He had never disagreed with my decisions because I had never spent money needlessly or frivolously.

I received a call from a friend of mine who knew both of us very well. She informed me that Rex had drawn $10,000.00 from our checking account and had been to our safe deposit box the day before his departure. Ten thousand dollars plus several credit cards should have paid for a nice little vacation.

As I look back on the blind trust I had in him, I feel like the fool I was. It was several days before I realized that he had taken everything out of our safe deposit box except my birth certificate and my passport. We had always kept several thousand dollars in cash in that safe deposit box along with stock certificates and insurance policies.

The laws of this land are generally skewed in favor of the criminal and deceitful beings. When assets such as ours are transferred to a foreign bank, that institution's only responsibility to our courts is to verify that an account does actually exist under an assigned number; no other information is required of that foreign bank. Rex, with 45 years of banking experience was well aware of that stipulation. This is the same man who had been my banker for 13 years before we married. I had trusted him with my life and every possession. As I look back in retrospect, I realize how truly naïve I was—so much so as to be considered stupid. Some of my friends who have known me for a lifetime remind me that I've never lived a normal life—somehow I've managed to always be on a pedestal of sorts. I made the choices always to take the high road and to associate only with very nice people. I have no "street smarts" which many of my friends find amusing. I finally began to realize that Rex could so out maneuver me when it came to finances.

Rex finally called me after being gone for 23 days. He told me that he had run into a donkey in Mexico and needed to buy a new car. He gave me names of dealers to call regarding makes and models of cars to price and to get back to him so he would know how to negotiate price with dealers in Laredo, Texas. Remember that he had always held that trump card of Mr. Smith, the banker, and never hesitated to play it. He was, however, out of his element and was obviously not thinking rationally. In that initial conversation, he said that the car was drivable, that he had some teenage boys finish breaking the windshield out of his car and that he had driven for four hours in a rain storm through August heat until he arrived in Laredo, Texas, back on American soil. To this day, I believe and always will, that there probably was a man on the donkey he hit. Whether the man was killed or horribly injured, I have no way of knowing. I do know that Rex wanted desperately to get out of Mexico.

His plan was to buy a new car, desert the wrecked car and simply leave it in Laredo. I suggested to him that he needed to notify the insurance company and finally convinced him to let me do so. It just so happened that the adjuster was in the local insurance office the next morning and he arranged a conference call between him, Rex, and me. He was able to make Rex realize that he needed to repair the absolute basics on that car and drive it back to Alabama so the insurance company could make an evaluation and settlement. It took three days and about two thousand dollars to repair the car enough to drive it home. The other repairs were made after he returned to Alabama.

He also asked if he could come home. After telling me that he had not had a drink or Prozac for ten days and that he would not have any more, ever again, if I would agree to let him come home. I had prepared myself for this moment. His behavior had, to me, been so bizarre and irrational that I felt certain he had a brain tumor. I told him that he could come home on condition of having a brain scan done upon arrival. He agreed and I was able to have that scan scheduled for the morning after he arrived home. His first remark to me upon returning was that he had made a terrible mistake and wanted our marriage to work out. My response was not what he expected. I told him that I was not willing to continue unless he had a verifiable brain disorder that could account for his irrationality. And that he would enter a rehab program to get off all drugs and alcohol.

I do believe that his realization that he had finally pushed me to the brink was actually a surprise to him. If he did have a medical problem I would certainly take care of him. Otherwise, he would have to accept that he had destroyed my love and trust for him and that I would not continue this marriage.

As he was unloading the car I discovered that he had a briefcase full of "street Prozac" and I was reminded that an addict will lie, cheat, and steal to get his fix. He had just given me the exclamation point I needed to complete my sentence. Yes! I would divorce him, no matter what!

Image and other's impression of him had always been a priority for him. Because of that I had imagined that I would stay in our house. After all, my parents had given us the land on which it was built. This property had been homesteaded by my ancestors. I had designed the house, hired the contractor and worked closely with all who had any part in building our house. The current owners of that house have told me that my spirit was still there when they moved in. I think one of the reasons Rex finally sold the house was that my signature was on every inch of every room. My personality pervaded everything. Rex actually thought that my many emotional ties to that property would never allow me to leave. Survival instinct far outweighs emotional ties.

My decision to leave was difficult and very far reaching. The ripples others experienced were anything but enjoyable but they had to be accepted. I knew what I had to do. Finally, there was a new voice I recognized as my own. I was determined to do the only thing I could do—determined to save the only life I could—mine! Suddenly, I took my heart in my hands and began the walk through an invisible wall into a new life. Rather than a decision, it was more of a recognition of whose time had come. Everything in my life was about to change. This kind of knowing just happens. Perhaps this seems too dramatic; to leave everything behind and strike out into unknown territory. When the time is right, only a small nudge is needed to make one fall headlong into a life that has been waiting all along.

I had to take that first step—just knowing that I needed to was not enough—I had to begin the journey. My mind was quiet with a tender certainty of truth that I had known always but was afraid to identify until now. My despair, loss and grief had to be left behind. A new beginning always follows a death of some sort. I became a new and different person and was no longer who I thought I was. I had to start the journey into an unknown world and knew that the choice was mine and mine alone. I had to leave everything familiar.

# HERA

The goddess Hera symbolizes air and the universe. After many years in a stifling if not suffocating marriage, I needed air, fresh air, and a lot of it. That need prompted me to treat myself to a lovely statue and fountain—something I could enjoy every day and while doing so, breathe very deeply sighs of relief.

Anyone who has lived with a controlling person understands all too well the desire to escape that heavy burden. The weighty load comes on slowly and over a long period of time. In the beginning it is indiscernible and is quite often interpreted as protectionism. By the time one realizes the truth of the matter, it is usually too late to bow out gracefully. It was twenty plus years before I had the strength and courage to admit to myself that I could no longer exist under this pressure. To realize that nothing changes until something changes is a step all co-dependent people must take in order to begin the long journey to recovery.

Late one afternoon in early summer 1996, I became so painfully aware of how sick I was. My husband was in bed, as he had been for several days, seeking refuge from his depression. I had worked in the rose garden until it was so dark I could no longer see well enough to do the occasional weeding, pruning, deadheading, etc. necessary to keep the roses healthy and in bloom. I went in to bathe and as I stood naked in the whirlpool bath which adjoined our bedroom by French doors, I realized that the pistol which always lay on top of a chest by his side of the bed was not in its usual place. In my bare, naked being I thought, *If he shoots me, I'll at least be clean.* At that very moment I knew it was time to do something I'd rarely allowed myself to even think—I had to remove myself from him or I would die at his hand.

I had hidden (or at least thought I had) the facts of our relationship from everyone—my mother, his daughters, our friends so well that I had no one with whom to share my pain. This was a defining moment in my life. For the first time, I knew that my only ally was GOD and that he knew where my heart was. From that moment, until this very day, I know I can do anything with His help. Somehow, some way, I made many right moves and decisions but it was as if I did them by remote control—and that's what it felt like to me at the time. I had always professed to let God into my life and thought I had until I finally gave my life to him.

I spent that night in the basement and never went to sleep. Rex went to a friend's the next morning on the pretense of going fishing. As soon as he was out of our driveway, I got dressed and drove to Montgomery. On the way there, I telephoned a friend who was an attorney and head of the Insurance Commission and asked him to recommend an attorney who would represent me in the divorce. My choice was greatly limited as most of the attorneys in Montgomery were connected to Rex, either through the bank where he had been employed for forty-five years or through personal friendship, or both. My friend was able to suggest a young, yet capable lawyer, Tony King. He was able to see me that morning and on looking back, I truly can't imagine what his first impression of me must have been. I was, needless to say, a huge bundle of nerves and so emotional, it was very difficult for me to talk without crying. But talk I did. His immediate recommendation was divorce. To protect financial interests, there was no other choice. In my naiveté, I did not realize that Rex's vindictiveness would begin the moment the "D" word was mentioned. Mr. King began the process and advised me not to leave our home. Little did I know that Rex was concerned only with his comforts and cared not a whit for mine. I could no longer exist under the same roof with him. And since he would not move out, I had no choice but leave.

After leaving Rex, I had no desire for another man in my life. He had been enough "man" to last any woman a lifetime. His demanding, totally consuming personality left me so drained of energy, that I felt totally hollow—empty. Recovery was going to be slow and tedious. Physical rest was absolutely essential in the beginning. For almost two weeks after I left, I had laryngitis and was unable to utter a sound. I stayed in an out of town motel and slept almost around the clock, except for running out to get meals. Not being able to speak was a blessing in disguise—as I look back on that time. Only one friend knew where I was—my mother was told that I was safe and kept informed enough to know that I was okay. Since I couldn't speak, there was no way to discuss options or plans and get input from others. This gave me time to make decisions completely on my own—right or wrong, they would be mine. I committed to hold on to my integrity at all costs, to be the best I could be under the circumstances and to protect myself from Rex and his wrath. Little did I know what an uphill battle I was facing.

I was able to rent an apartment whose rental rate was based on income (what income?). My lease was dated October 1996. Mother provided a bed, linens, washer, dryer, and many incidentals; a friend brought over wicker pool furniture for my living room and dining area; another friend brought dishes, cookware, and stocked my cupboards and fridge with groceries. I have often heard it said that one will learn who their true friends are when going through a divorce. Much to my surprise, people came out of the woodwork to help me—people I didn't know cared about me. Their generosity helped to restore my faith in human beings and to realize that we are taken wherever God wants us to go.

I had never lived on my own until this time. I had lived with my parents until I married my first husband in 1965. Everyone, and I do mean everyone, needs to be totally dependent on themselves at some point in life. I just happened to have had this experience later in life than most. My spiritual growth is what I needed and of which I am most proud. I have a peace in my heart which is such a gift from God. The *worrying me* has become the *grateful me*. How I wish I had had this always!! I have continued to pray for Rex to find that same peace and ease his anger and hatred for others, especially for me. All of that anger must be so draining, such a waste of energy.

Within a week of moving into my small apartment, I sensed that I was being watched. Rex was always able to think like a criminal and my naiveté left me ill prepared to anticipate his moves and motives. An employee of the apartment complex kept him informed of my coming and goings. On Sunday mornings while I was at church, someone would enter my apartment and place listening devices on my phone and answering machine. In the beginning, I attributed my uneasiness to paranoia, but after replacing several answering machines, my attorney decided to hire a private investigator without advising me that he had done so. The PI had reported to him that I had on a navy and white suit. I confirmed that I was indeed dressed as the PI had described and was on my way to church. He told me that the PI would be on duty sporadically. On that first day, an employee of the complex went up a ladder at the back of my apartment and was then seen walking around in my living room. This scenario was repeated the following two Sunday mornings. At this point, we knew that my uneasiness was more that paranoia.

Several of my friends and I went to the High Museum in Atlanta to see the Dali exhibit. I noticed that someone appeared to be following me soon after I left my apartment that morning. After a few maneuvers, I was certain I was being followed and called ahead to tell my friends what was going on. They had the charter bus driver ready to drive away as soon as I boarded the bus in Montgomery. It was not long before the driver told us that we were, indeed, being followed. That individual tailed us all day and followed me back to my apartment that night. I went inside, locked my door, and put on my security chain. As soon as I kicked off my shoes, I realized that the carpet in my living room was wet. On further inspection, I found that my kitchen and laundry areas were also wet. There had been a terrible thunderstorm with high winds during that afternoon while I was in Atlanta. I spent quite a while throwing out all the boxes of dry ingredients (laundry detergent, cereals, ect.) and cleaning up the mess as best I could. On Monday morning, the apartment manager sent someone over to check out my situation. There were no leaking hoses or anything to cause this much water to be in my area. The repair guy brought in a ladder so that he could go into the attic to investigate further. I was standing by the ladder when he opened the access cover to the attic. We were both shocked to see blue sky above us. When the storm winds were so strong on Saturday afternoon, they had lifted a cut out section of roof and left the hole into my attic exposed to the elements and to intruders. I could not believe my eyes! The rain had been very heavy—heavy enough to wet a big portion of my apartment. I now I had proof of how strangers were invading my space.

Since I had already found my house at Rural Home, I began sleeping there the next night. I had nothing but my bed there because so much work had to be done before I could actually move in. I felt that I was safer anywhere than in that apartment!

The chapter entitled TRUST will make you question my safety delusion!

# SPECIAL RELATIONSHIPS

Friendships are cyclical and some are longer than others. People come into our lives at exactly the right time. Some friends have been in my life for almost as long as I can remember and reminiscing with them brings joy and pleasure as well as sorrow. Re-visiting childhood events, early adulthood trials and my Daddy is therapeutic. I wish that I had recorded Daddy telling stories since he was a master at that—so much so that for as long as he lived, I would ask my mother if what he said was *a truth or a tale.*

One of my friends has no idea how truly funny she can be. She is shy and demure but always makes me laugh. She is always well dressed, make-up and hair perfect and is truly beautiful, inside and out. She's the only person I know who does her hair before going to the beauty shop. Lately, her husband has had several health problems, so before washing and rolling her hair, she checks with him to see if an emergency room visit is eminent. If he's feeling poorly, she *puts on her face* and does her hair before going to bed while sleeping sitting up! She's the only new mother I've ever known who put on make-up before letting her husband see her after the birth of a baby. That's my dear friend Linda!

Her grandmother would always remind her of the starving children in China and encourage her to eat everything on her plate. As she says,

*It didn't do them one bit of good; they're still skinny and I'm the one who got fat!*

She has also told her gynecologist that she would prefer that neither he nor his nurse be in the room for her annual examination. Perhaps her suggestion will encourage him to create a robot so none of us will have to suffer that indignity!

Another friend was on her way to our house early one morning and sped through a thirty-five mile per hour zone at fifty-five miles per hour. Almost immediately blue lights and siren were beside her. She continued on a bit before pulling over. When the policeman questioned her actions, she told him she was giving him the benefit of doubt, just in case he was after someone else. Her ticket was eighty-five dollars!

We have a friend whose brother works for the state prison system. Her mother is a telephone dispatcher for the county sheriff's department and her sister is a nurse. Our friend is the welcoming face and first person contact at a local physical rehabilitation facility. When asked about his family, her father is quick to explain that his son is in *prison*, his wife is in *jail*, one of his daughters *pushes drugs* and his other daughter is in *rehab*. It's all a matter of interpretation!

During my lifetime I have been more than fortunate to have wonderful help. When I was a child, we had Edna and Trixie; both were live-in housekeepers and baby sitters. I still remember how Edna smelled, always pristine in her dress and hygiene—just so clean she smelled sweet. Trixie, on the other hand, was a very large woman and less careful about personal cleanliness. Trixie would take weekends off and quite often would not return to work until Tuesday. It was very common for her to have a headache or stomachache which always cured itself after a good nights' sleep. She *smelled the cork* a few too many times while visiting her friends on weekends. But I loved her dearly—she was the one who could pick me up and carry me around when I couldn't walk. It was not difficult for her to put me in the tub or bed or load me in the car.

After I was married, I had many people clean for me but the most memorable one was Mary. She had been a pastry chef for one of the local cafeterias in Montgomery and taught me a lot about cooking. She was great at ironing and I would have kept her forever if I'd had the chance.

There have been several vacuum cleaners in my life—most of which I didn't know how to turn on. Since I've always been involved in other endeavors, my housekeeper had to be good. It isn't that I mind housekeeping; I'd just rather be doing other things. But, my house must be clean. If it's a mess, so am I.

My help, both domestic and yard, become like family to us. They are so well trained and capable that I need only to tell them what's needed and they can proceed.

I realize how very fortunate I am to have employees who stay with me for years and one in particular comes to mind. When I would go on trips I would return home to floors which had been stripped and waxed, every dish washed and in its place in the cabinet, clean linens on my bed and if at the appropriate time of year, the house would be beautifully decorated for Christmas. He was the kind of person who could be in the house accomplishing all kinds of chores but at the same time being as quiet as a church mouse. He was also a wonderful cook who served beautifully. And yet, could keep the lawn perfectly manicured and flower beds weed free. One of the greatest losses in my life was losing this *jack* of all trades and *master* of most. For years people had tried to tell me that he was homosexual. I must admit to my homophobia. Even after he left his wife and children and moved in with a *boyfriend* I still would not and could not accept this as fact. Now, in hindsight, I know that I was simply in denial. I finally asked him if he was homosexual and without saying a word, he dropped his head, picked up his hat and walked out my door. Losing him was harder than losing my ex-husband by divorce. A few months after he left, his significant other died. When I saw this wonderful man recently, he looked very, very thin and drawn.

My husband and I count our blessings daily and very near the top of the list are Gilbert and Mitch. We have a beautiful yard and home and these two men work very hard to make us look good.

Mitch is a success story of which I'm very proud. About twenty-five years ago a neighbor brought Mitch to me since he had nothing for him to do. I did not realize that he was a full-fledged drug head at the time. I'd never been exposed to anyone who used street drugs so the symptoms were not evident to me. He was about thirty, had never been married, lived with his mother, did not have a car or driver's license and needed to be paid every afternoon when I took him home or dropped him off in town. He wore the same clothes 2 or 3 days in a row and would come to work in the yard with no shoes. I'd buy him shoes and a day or so later he'd be barefoot again. When questioned about where his shoes were, he'd tell me someone stole his shoes while he was sleeping or some other lame excuse. I, being the fool I was, would go buy him more shoes as well as shirt and pants. He never had a dime—no matter how much I paid him. Finally, he was arrested and jailed for possessing drugs and paraphernalia and for forging a stolen check.

While in jail, he was persuaded to straighten out his life and live the way his mother and the rest of his family had begged him to do for years. I would always encourage Mitch and tell him that he was wasting his life—that he could do so much better. I never gave up on him but had my doubts regarding his recovery. I only knew that he was in jail but had no further information about him. About 3 years later he came to me while I was shopping and asked if he could work for me again. He was with his mother and sister and looked like a different person. He had gained weight, was clean and neat and looked me in the eye when we talked. This was ten years ago and Mitch has never been late or not shown up on time or lied to me since. He is a happy, confident man who has a wife, a good job, has bought a house, owns several vehicles and is a member of a well-known singing group. He does all he can to inspire others to live a drug-free life. I am very proud of Mitch and remind him regularly of that fact.

Gilbert is our miracle! He was stricken with throat cancer about 14 years ago. His youngest child was about 3 months old at the time of his diagnosis. His wife and young children moved on with their lives and left him all alone to fight the battle of his life. He did just that and has proven himself to be victorious. He came to help a friend of his weed eat our yard. I was able to understand Gilbert when he was just learning to use his voice box. I was so impressed with his effort and work ethic that I asked him to work more and more. He has a key to our house and simply does what needs to be done without supervision. What a gift he is to us!

Gilbert is a very nice looking man who is quite the dresser. He is also a collector of vintage cars. He is much more than an employee, he is family to us and we love him like the brother he is.

I have learned that anyone can be available when times are good. But the biggest test comes when the weather becomes foul. These friends are here for us, no matter what.

# CONTRACT WITH DADDY

My father was a very strong-willed, outspoken, often times difficult person but he had a heart of gold and was hiding the teddy bear he really was.

He and I were very close and my entire family expected me to be the negotiator between them and him. I could always talk him into giving my sisters permission to go places or to do things that were out of the ordinary. When he and mother were at a crossroads in their relationship, I was usually the one who would smooth out the wrinkles. This continued right up until his death.

After I married and left home, my dad became very depressed and so difficult that my mother could not deal with him. I personally had him committed to the psych ward at an out of town hospital so he could receive the help he so desperately needed. I visited him every day but his anger at me was so great that he did not acknowledge me or speak to me for over three weeks—even though I went to see him every day. Through lots of professional help and prayers, he finally came around and returned to the loving father I had always known. For as long as he lived, he would relapse from time to time but his bouts with depression and anxiety were never as severe as that first one.

Daddy was a smoker in his earlier years, as were most men in his generation. He, however, paid a tremendous price for that vice and suffered from COPD, asthma, and emphysema the last twenty years of his life. Any one of these conditions would have been too much to live with, but all three made it almost impossible to survive in this climate. His inability to breath and the unpredictability of those attacks contributed greatly to his almost constant state of angst. He was, by his very nature, impatient and anxious. My mother was, for a very long time, his primary caregiver, wife, and life line. She took her jobs very seriously and probably held up under the strain of his ill health and temperament as well as anyone in the world could have. On occasion, he could be so difficult that she would have to have a break. His local physician was very much attuned to both of them and I shall be forever grateful to him for his kindnesses and professional handling of this great difficulty.

On Daddy's last long stay in the hospital, where he died, he became very difficult and demanding, even as sick as he was. Mother was so exhausted by this time that I had to take the lead role in his care for the family. She would sit with him for a few hours in the late afternoons and evenings, a private-duty nurse would stay with him overnight and remain with him until I took my shift the next morning. I had a home and husband to maintain as well. Early in this stint of sickness, I arrived at Daddy's room, which was situated directly across from the nurse's station. On entering his room, he spoke very harshly to me and I deemed that this was going to be an extremely long day for me. I never took my purse off my arm and told Daddy that I would not be treated unkindly by him or anyone else; that I would return at the same time the next day and that I was going home to give him some "alone" time to sweeten his disposition. As I walked out of his room and out the door of that hospital, I cried, however, never letting him see. By the time I arrived home, he had left several messages for me and had called mother to *tell on me*. I spent the rest of that day with her so she would not go down to humor him as she almost always gave in to his whims.

The next day, as I entered his room, I expected the environment to be different, but it was not! He was unable to contain his anger and lashed out again! Again, I picked up my purse and explained that I would be back the next day, same time, to check on his attitude. If acceptable, I would stay the day with him. If he was rude, he could be assured that I would leave again.

By the third day, when I entered his room, my contract with him had been signed, sealed and delivered. His demeanor let me know that my contract was very binding. Over the next six-weeks, his final days on this earth, he and I were able to handle many of his private affairs which he had neglected to do. We were also able to quietly and peacefully discuss some things which he needed to share.

Until I made that contract with my father, he did not seen to realize that he could no longer be in charge of the mundane, nor did he need to be. That responsibility had to be transferred to those of us who were able-bodied. He was a bright man, strong-willed and his strength of mind served him well until the end. It was much easier to give Daddy up after having had our final discussions. I thank him daily for his many gifts to me and for going peacefully to a much more wonderful place.

Many of my friends, who have aging parents, are terribly frustrated by their parents' inability to let go and allowing their children to take care of their needs. I hear horror stories about parents who are apparently of sound mind but behave as spoiled children. I view parent-caring as a way to repay some of what we owe them for giving us life and all the continued care it took to mold us into the adult we are today. I was fortunate enough to be able to choose to move back, near my parents, when they needed me most. I have never regretted that personal decision and have had no tears of guilt. However, giving them up has left a void in my life which only parents can fill.

Contracting with difficult people, no matter what the relationship, has worked for me many times. Once we realize that our personal choices are just that, choices, but the effects of those decisions are far-reaching and can make our lives and the lives of others either a heaven or hell on earth.

# LIFE BEGINS AT 50

Human beings, by changing their attitudes can change the outer aspects of their lives. We must realize that everyone's life journey is just as difficult, if not more difficult, than ours. Everyone is on the same road. We are never alone. And sometimes the best things in life take place when we do what we should do rather than what we feel like doing.

Fifty is magical, or it was for me. I finally realized that in my pitiful little way, I had climbed the mountains I had chosen. In the midst of a very troublesome divorce, God gave me a peace I had never known before. It was as if I was beginning anew but, this time, with a knowledge that would make climbing mountains feel only like going uphill. I learned that laughter feels really good and that there's a lot of tangible evil in this world. I learned also that the earth will keep on turning and that there is such a great peace in nature. I learned that beauty is very healing and good for the spirit and we must surround ourselves with as much of it as possible. And furthermore, that there is no such thing as a free lunch. The only person I need to impress is me!

During the months following my fiftieth birthday I asked myself—

*What have I done?*

*How did I do it?*

*Where did I mess up?*

*What have I done well?*

After assessing my life, I realized that I had brought a lot of joy to many people. I had been a good daughter. I had tried to be a good wife. I had been to foreign lands and had met many very interesting people. And I got _it_! I was not helpless or lost and I had not the right to give up on myself. As alone as I was, I had the best consultants in the world—my head and my heart. They assured me that my values would continue to be set by the choices I made—hour by hour, day by day, over a lifetime. The only time I needed to be happy was in this moment. It is truly miraculous to realize the totality of who we are. We are much more than our body and certainly much more than our body image. After I learned to love the skin I'm in I also learned to use paper plates and napkins. This is tremendous progress for a lady who had always set a formal table with linen napkins. I didn't feel the need to learn to sky dive or drive a motorcycle or read Greek because if I haven't learned those things by now, maybe I shouldn't or needn't. This, after all, is when I'm supposed to be settling in and behaving sensibly. I said *supposed* to be.

Our inner beauty supersedes all else and keeps us connected to our consciousness. No time is wasted with my wondering if I am worthy of a good day but knowing that I am entitled to a great day! If I allow myself to be open to the concerns of others, their hopes and fears, and can make them feel less alone and abandoned, I are the epitome of humanity. When I carry the load for another human being, that is love in the truest sense.

Pain can actually bring us closer to the truth. If I stay the course and touch the rareness of a painful experience, I can learn from it. If I choose not to absorb that experience, I will lose my compassion and empathy for others. Quite often, denial of actual circumstances is our own false pride and ego. I need to taste it, smell it and experience it completely in order to grow. I must have an appetite for life as it is rather than life as I want it to be. Living in the moment allows me to be happier, more balanced and more compassionate. Once I realized that happiness and success are journeys, not destinations, I became more gracious. Just being alive in this moment is success.

Happy people are that way because they choose to be happy. Unhappy people are that way because they choose to be unhappy. *Fears, worry, anger, sorrow, jealousy, self-pity, resentment*, and *inferiority* all lead to unhappiness. *Joy, love, hope, serenity, kindness, generosity, truth*, and *compassion* equate happiness. Healthy, supportive relationships are more precious than jewels.

My life's philosophy is still developing and I hope to share more with you in future writings. But at this point, I am sure there will be joyful purpose in all that I do.

# REPUTATION VS. CHARACTER

Reputation is what *others think* of us. Character is what *we know* about us. Our values guide every decision we make, and therefore, our destiny. Decision making for me has never been difficult and I attribute that to the fact that there is little "gray" in my life. I live in a black and white world on a daily basis and have a definite opinion on almost every subject.

A few years ago my nephew brought his beautiful new girlfriend to visit. She was very impressive on first meeting because of her physical beauty and gorgeous smile. He left her to visit with me, one on one, while I finished making dinner. As is my habit, I asked very general questions regarding her family, school, likes, dislikes, etc. It seemed that no matter what I asked, her stock answer was, "Well, I never thought about that!" The old adage that *beauty is only skin deep* was certainly true in this case!

I was fortunate to have parents who expected me to do the right things always and my values were established early on and I learned discipline and confidence and determination. If we are not clear about what we stand for, how will we ever develop a sense of self-esteem? Once our value system is truly clarified, decision making becomes simple. Living a life where our actions and philosophies are one is often times an enviable state. We must live by our highest values and ideals in order to be fulfilled. We have the ability to design our destiny and to dictate who we become. If our character is what it should be, our reputations should be excellent.

Reputations, however, can be misrepresented by individuals who are envious, jealous or rumor mongers. The gossip mill is alive and well and will continue to be. We must rise above that pettiness and continue to refine our character as God intended us to do. With His help, we can be whoever we want to be and accomplish more than we ever imagined. *He* never asks for more that we give!

Most of our decisions aren't made in order to grow or explore life but are all about self-preservation and security. Many times we don't aim to win; we simply don't want to lose. When we make our major decisions to please, appease or somehow meet the needs of everyone—except ourselves, we are selling ourselves short. Peer pressure continues long after adolescence if we allow ourselves to make our decisions in life only to please others. We must think of ourselves. We are limited only by our own expectations. We should strive for much more than *survival*—we should aim for *thrival*.

# STEP PARENTING

More than any other job, I think parenting, when done properly, must be the most demanding of all. I never had the privilege of being a parent but have been married twice to men who had children from previous marriages. There appears to be an innate desire of children of divorce to want their biological parents to be together again. It does not seem to matter that they and their parents were miserable when they were together.

Step parenting for me has been like having a big toe in a very icy pool, constantly testing the water. I always stand firmly on my principles but tread very lightly in the hope of not stepping on anyone's toes. Is that why it's called "step-parenting." I grew up watching step parenting in motion.

My mother was married to Charlie Herman Cauthen who died from gangrene after being kicked by a horse. Mother gave birth to my sister Britt three months after his death. Three years later, my mother and father married and they had my sister Julie and me.

Britt was a beautiful child, almost doll-like in the pictures I remember. She was seven years older than I and I held her in very high esteem while growing up. As a small child, I recognized that Britt was special—especially to my father.

He treated her differently than he treated his biological children. She could do no wrong so far as he was concerned. She was allowed privileges Julie and I would have dared request.

My father's expectations of us were extreme—after all, we were his children. It was perfectly acceptable if Britt made less than perfect grades and didn't excel on all attempted challenges. His partiality to her was obvious to others as well. He always seemed to overcompensate on every level where Britt was concerned.

Mother spent her entire life loving Charlie Herman. My father's strong personality and healthy ego somehow enabled him to compete with a dead man. On looking back, I am awed by his endurance. Daddy's personality was very strong and fun-loving and he could usually lift Mother's heavy seriousness. There was always a thread of sadness that was a part of her. As an adult, I have reasoned that this could have been caused by the loss of her first love. And as I have grown, I know that we each deal with grief and loss in our own unique manner. I did learn from her that life is not really about the plans we have for ourselves—life is NOW. Life must be enjoyed rather than endured.

# THE GIFT THAT KEEPS
# ON GIVING

Every little boy needs a dog! Every human, so far as I can tell, needs a dog! I have been more blessed than most in that I have had two very fine dogs that I miss until this day.

Lady D was the most beautiful dog I've ever seen, both physically and in personality. She was one of my greatest gifts. Her father, Duke was a wedding gift to Rex and me. He was very spoiled, did not want me to have anything to do with other dogs, and was downright rude to any and all four-legged creatures who ever tried to get near me. He was the only dog I've ever known who would help weed the garden! I would take him with me when weeding or working in the garden and he would try to do whatever I was doing. He would actually grasp the weeds with his teeth, pull them out of the ground and put them in a pile! For as long as I stayed in the garden, he was right by my side. One day, he and I had a long discussion regarding other dogs. I assured him that as long as he lived, I would never get another pet and I kept my word to him. He, however, did not honor our agreement. A beautiful Irish setter mix lady dog came to visit him one day and her pedigree, or lack thereof, did not seem important to him. He thought she was gorgeous, so much so that after a few minutes of courtship, they decided to get married! When the ceremony was over, I called Rex to tell him Duke had chosen a wife and we would soon be grandparents. We called her Duchess since every duke needs his lady of honor. Duke had a nose so long that he actually had difficulty eating and his allergies were a constant bother. A lot of grains of pollen could find their way into that nose of his. His coloring was grand but his hair was always very coarse. While Duchess was carrying his babies, I prayed that one of them would have a nose not nearly so long as Duke's nose, that its hair would have the texture of its mother's and that it would be female. When she had her first pup, out of a litter of nine, my order had been filled to perfection. Lady D became my dog. Duke had become a father and did not mind having his daughter live with us. We found Duchess and the eight other litter mates very good homes. Duke proved to be a fine father and was patient and attentive to Lady D. She was born mid-March and was adjusting to her human and dog families. In July, Duke lost a few pounds and seemed a bit lethargic. Within a week, he was obviously very sick. I took him to the vet, who had treated him for years and he found that he had worms; two little pills would take care of that and I could take him back home. Something within me said that there was more to Duke's malaise than worms. I asked the vet to humor me and keep him overnight for observation. He assured me that Duke would be fine. The next morning when he was tending the cages of his patients, he found Duke dead! He told me months later that the call to notify me was the hardest call he ever had to make to a client. An autopsy revealed that Duke had died of renal failure. Duke had loved and been loved for nine years and had left a beautiful daughter to carry on his name. And did she ever! Anyone who knew me knew Lady D.

*The litter of nine.*

*Lady D*

When Lady D was about three, a friend sent me a male rat terrier who we named Bobo. He weighed all of a pound when he arrived, in a shoe box. Lady D, by this time, was about 85 pounds of gorgeous dog. It was evident from Bobo's first night at home that he would be the dominant one of this pair. This never changed, not for a moment.

She tolerated him and became more and more attached to me. Bobo certainly was worth his keep because nothing moved or was moved without his noticing it. He rode with us on short trips to the grocery store or cleaners and was always the first in the car. The rear dash was his favorite spot because it allowed him to see everything. After he was outside, I would purposely move a chair, a cushion, or put something on the floor—anything that would be different than when he had walked out the door. He would, invariably, go straight to whatever was different and go into full alert mode as soon as we returned home. He was a wonderful watch dog.

But he developed a very testy attitude. He had very short legs and was broad and muscular. He was aloof and extremely quick to anger. Snapping and biting were very natural to him.

When I left Rex, I moved into a small apartment—no pets allowed. I felt certain Rex would at least be good to the dogs. The only way he could really hurt my heart by this time was by mistreating Lady D. Bobo would not tolerate abuse and bit Rex on more than one occasion—once when he was feeding him candy but not unwrapping it fast enough!

After I moved to Rural Home, almost a year after leaving Rex, he had one of the men who worked for me bring Lady D to me. She obviously had been neglected for that entire time. Her coat was so matted that she had to be shaved completely. She went to the vet early on Monday and I was told that she had a terrible urinary tract infection. She had to be wormed and given all her vaccinations because there was no way to know what Rex had done for her—if anything. When I picked her up from the groomer with her clean-shaven body, she had numerous skin lesions which took some time to heal. She was so embarrassed to be *naked*. Her coat grew back to be as beautiful as ever, so much so that when I would take her for walks, passersby would stop their cars just to look at her. Tri-colored collies are not a common breed in this area.

On the Sunday she was delivered to me, we held on to each other all day. I was so happy to have my beautiful girl with me again. It was obvious that she had really missed me too. Only people who have been separated from a pet and then reunited can understand that special bond which is much stronger the second time around. The attachment I had to this huge ball of fur defies description. She is the only dog I've ever known who always smelled good. She never had a *doggy* smell and at 95 pounds was a house dog.

She lost her sight and hearing but was still able to function very well. She and I did everything on schedule and had few problems until her arthritis began to make getting up and down almost impossible. I would stand over her, put my hands under her belly and lift her to standing position; steadying her between my knees until she could take a few steps. She was then able to walk outside and go to the bathroom. All went well until I broke my arm. My friends who knew her well were taking care of both of us. She, however, would not let them lift her as I did. I soon realized that God had me break my arm so I'd make the decision to let her suffer no longer. And, so I could cry a lot over the next three months. Duke's decision to become a *family man* gave me almost 14 years of utter joy in Lady D.

I have a wonderfully unselfish niece who gave me her six-year-old rat terrier, who came from a line of very dainty delicate terriers with a sweet, sweet disposition. She loved Precious so much but when her son became old enough to crawl, my niece realized that she had her hands a bit too full with two babies in the house. She drove her to me and when Carla went upstairs to the guest bedroom, we all expected Precious to sleep with her. She went up in Carla's arms but as I was crawling into bed, Precious was at my feet. I thought that if I ignored her she would go back upstairs to be with my niece. She decided that night that she wanted to sleep with me and did so every night except those she spent at the wonderful Dr. Joe Maddox's vet clinic or traveled with our friend, Lois.

She had the cutest disposition and personality I've ever seen in a dog. She was constant joy and entertainment. When she was here, I did a lot of entertaining of groups—garden clubs, civic clubs, bridal teas and luncheons—groups as small at 8 to 10 or as large as two hundred. She always had good manners and had the innate ability to find the best lap in the crowd. She has been listed as a guest at many business meetings of garden and civic clubs. People who didn't like dogs loved Precious.

For some reason, still unknown to me, she wanted no one to go into the bathroom of my mom's apartment except Mother or me. After Mother went to live in the nursing home, I converted that area to a sunroom which is where we spend most of our time.

Gene left the kitchen table to go to that bathroom one morning and Precious began barking and nipping at his heels. I raised my voice to her, for the first time, and she was so shocked by my tone that she dropped her ears, picked up one foot and began limping as though she had been hit! I'm glad I have him as a witness to her reaction!

She loved to watch birds and squirrels from the windows of the sunroom and was barking incessantly one day. Gene popped her with a folded sheet of newspaper and told her to hush. She continued barking but came running to me, nudged her way under my arm with only her head sticking out and continued to fuss at him. She considered me her protector.

Our neighbor across the highway had two Australian shepherds who he would anchor to pecan trees in his front yard. His male dog was very vocal and would bark aggressively any time Precious and I went outside. One day as I took her outside, she did not turn right as was her habit but went straight up the walkway, as close as she could get to his male dog and barked in a very sharp little voice. When she finished speaking to him, she scratched with her front feet, then back feet, turned around and came back inside. I think I now understand the meaning of *dog cussing* since I've seen it happen. Rye never barked again when Precious and I went out the front door.

I had a neighbor whose voice was a bit raspy and harsh. She spoke more loudly than Gene or I did. Almost every time she came for a visit, she would sit in the kitchen and Precious would get directly under her chair. The only time I was aware that Precious passed gas was when she was right under this lady. Precious was very consistent in this naughty behavior and saved it all for my neighbor's visits, and needless to say, her visits were usually brief.

Rat terriers are known to be very loyal to one person in a family but Precious seemed to love both of us. When Gene would come home from work or errands, Precious would sometimes be in the front yard going to the bathroom. The moment he pulled into the driveway, she would stop everything—even in mid-stream—so she could run back inside, through the house and be at the back door to greet him. It never mattered to her that he often had on a black or charcoal suit. Those little white hairs are hard to remove from dark fabrics. She expected him to pick her up and love on her before he could speak to me.

Gilbert, our gardener and friend, has a key to our house and watches over things for us when we have to be away. We had gone to Canton, Georgia, to do an arts and crafts show and he was taking care of Precious for us. When Gene and I were home and Gilbert would come over, Precious would greet him at the back door with barking that would make us think a total and complete stranger was there. However, Gilbert told us that when we were not at home, she would greet him with a tail wagging, totally quiet demeanor saved for only her favorite people! On Saturday afternoon when he came over to check on and walk her, she did not greet him as usual. He walked through the house, calling to her and got no response. He went upstairs to see if she was in her bed by my desk but still did not find her. He knew that she was supposed to be inside but he could not find her anywhere. He went back to his house, all the while trying to figure what he would say when he called to tell us she was missing. Before making that call, he decided to come back over once more and search the house. As he entered the sunroom, he saw two little black ears sticking up between the cushion and rear of the sofa. She had nestled herself in a very cozy position and did not want to be disturbed from her peaceful sleep. Poor Gilbert had, by this time, worked himself into quite a frenzy of concern. I'm sure he felt like killing her but was so happy to find her that the thought soon dissipated. He still laughs when he recounts the story of looking for Precious.

There are people on this earth who can never have enough money or property or possessions. Precious was the dog who could never get enough *loving*. Let me assure you that she got lots of loving from us and everyone who knew her. Lois, a dear friend of ours, would dog-sit for us when we had to go out of town for meetings or exhibits. We would call to check on Precious and Lois would tell us they were in Birmingham or Montgomery or at the beach. They were the traveling duo. But, when Precious returned home, from her trips with Lois, she would be completely exhausted and would rest for the next week.

Precious had an internal clock that was as accurate as any atomic time piece in the world. She never minded when Gene went to work, shopping, fishing or whatever he wanted to do. I, on the other hand, would be ignored for equal amounts of time I was away from her, whether two hours or two days, she would pout with me. When that time elapsed she would return to her normal, sweet self.

We have a resident ghost dog who we think is also a rat terrier. The descendants of the man who built our house in 1916 have told us that their grandfather was known to love this breed of dogs. On occasion this entity came to play with Precious. When it was present, she would completely ignore my commands for her to come downstairs, so much so that I would have to go up and bring her down in my arms. Sometimes she would slip back upstairs and continue to bark and play. Carlotta and Tom, Gene's older children, have both been aware of the ghost dog when visiting. At this point we're not really sure if that spirit is Precious or her play mate but either way, we're glad to have them close by.

Since Precious's death, my husband and I have simply been unable to commit to another dog. We feel that getting a new puppy would be unfair to it, because we still feel that by comparison to Precious, any dog would pale. She was the truly perfect dog for us and we miss her so. Hardly a day passes that we don't mention her and her antics. She died over five years ago and when we come in the door we still subconsciously await her grand welcome. When Precious greeted us, we knew that all was well with this world! We were a totally complete little family in the safe cocoon of home!

# HAPPINESS

Material wealth has nothing to do with happiness. Happiness comes from giving, not getting. We are able to make those around us comfortable and happy only if we have attained enough comfort and happiness to be able to share with others. The more we love, the more we are loved. When we give with no thought of receiving, we automatically receive in abundance. If we are spiritually and psychologically mature, love and positive energy flow from us. Not a word must be said for others to share that feeling—we become a magnet to them.

My husband and I are very blessed with friends. God puts us where we need to be, at any given time. Interruptions are His way of changing our direction. Failures are His way of showing us that we need to make different choices.

Blessings abound in all shapes and sizes . . . a loving smile, a tender touch, a few moments of quiet. What a joy it is to celebrate the blessings in our lives knowing full well that God put them there! Expose others to them. Share. Live life to the fullest—all day, every day. This is the only trip through life we take; therefore, make the most of it! In order to blaze a new trail of life, we must let go of fear and hurt and pain from the past. It is sometimes easier to act our way into a new way of thinking than it is to think our way into a new way of acting.

# CAREGIVING

Overwhelmed. Exhausted. Heart sick. Anxious. Not feeling well. These are only a few of the things that permeated my life when I was caring for my mother, an Alzheimer's patient. As much as I loved her and wanted to take care of her, my capabilities were woefully inadequate. For three and a half years, I slept with one or both eyes open and lived with a constant fear that she would hurt herself. I rushed as much as the speed limits would allow and sometimes exceeded them in my haste to return to her, even though she was in the care of sitters, and pushed myself to the extreme—physically and emotionally. Words are totally inadequate when trying to describe how I felt as a caregiver. The following are actual, hand-written excerpts from my personal journal;

10/19/2000
Midnight

Doing mixed laundry - throw rug, pink pants and panties. At 11:30, I checked on Mother and she looked like a dead person - sleeping very soundly. I came back to my bed and dozed off. Was awakened by noise in her apartment. She was crouched by the refrigerator using the garbage can for a potty! Thought everything was O.K. - could take care of that in the morning. Got Mother a glass of water and when I started back to my bed I discovered that she had missed the garbage can and had wet the rug. She was coughing so I went back to her bed to check on her and found that she was wet. I helped her change and put her back to bed.

I took her to Dr. Smith today and he noticed her anemic color. Gave her ativan and keflex. She has a cold. We'll get her flu shot in a couple of weeks.

Mother was very "together" and rational while in doctor's office.

10/20/2000

Janie kept Mother this morning and accomplished some work as well. I'm so lucky to have her.

Nadine called with a list of possible sitters -- not a moment too soon.

After Janie left today, Mother went out to visit with her dogs. When she came back in, she began looking for her gun and did not find it. Came and asked if I knew where it was (I had removed it from her closet while she was outside). For the first time in my life, I lied to her and told her I did not know where it was. Her response was "that's what you say!" I feel so hollow lying to her but I must do this -- for her safety and mine. And when her vehicle does not start, I'll have to tell her another story. Gene Sykes disabled it for me. I have alerted her mechanic of this situation. If she cannot find her bed or the light switch in her bathroom (just a couple of examples) she does not need to be driving!!

I wish I had unlimited funds and could afford sitters around the clock but I can't. I will do my best for her. Realizing that I can't "fix" this or even make it better, is very painful for me. She is truly my baby at this time.

It's 2:15 AM and she's sleeping soundly

10/20/2000
11:20 P.M.

Mother just got up to go to the bathroom but had no idea where the bathroom was! She could not turn ~~on~~ the light. After wetting herself, she can back to her bedroom and pulled out several pairs of panties — put on one pair while standing — then sat down and tried to put on another pair. She rolled up her wet p.j's and panties and put them in a drawer. Poor, pitiful Mother! There is no light in her eyes. She has been quilting today and I know that this will be her last attempt.

She has always done such beautiful, perfect handwork but this would embarass her if she were not so ill. She still talks about all her projects and to someone who is not around her 24 hours a day, she appears lucid.

When Mother and I go for rides on the golf cart, she sees the roses, in her eyes, for the very first time — — even if she's seen them a dozen times that day. Simple pleasures mean so much!

I had a long conversation today with Mary Simon. She listened to me and made me feel not so alone. She has cared for her mother-in-law who has Alzheimers. She advised me to continue to journal even though I have not the time. I am crying as I write. My tears are so close to the surface — some must come out.

Later — Mother's up again. When I was getting her back to bed, she asked "where is the bed?" Poor soul — at a moment like that — when she is truly in another world, I know she needs to be in the nursing home. But, when she is lucid, she would be so upset. I'm not sure I'll be able to handle that emotionally. Just writing this brings more tears. Why is this so hard? I wish I could stop being so sad. Am tired of feeling so stressed. Most of the time I feel sick — like really sick!

This was the second time I had been responsible for an elderly Alzheimer's patient. The first one was my ex-husband's mother but it was very different than when it became my mother. The emotional ties I felt for her multiplied the responsibility exponentially. Not having children of my own might have made this responsibility harder for me to accept. I was used to having the freedom to do whatever I liked whenever I liked and for the first time in my life, I was totally responsible for another human being's total care. By the time Mother came to live with me, I was beyond the denial stage and knew that her condition would only worsen. As much as I hate to say this to others who are going where I have been, the good days become fewer and the bad days come more often. Understanding that the disease limits capabilities and the ability to cope with everyday issues helps caregivers to manage the disease more easily. But, I can assure anyone brave enough and responsible enough to care for your loved one, it is a decision you will look back on with the wonderful feeling of knowing you did the right thing! Leave the guilt to those who could have and didn't. Your grief will come in stages in all probability. The first stage of mine was while Mother was with me and I was not able to make her *happy*. She did not know what she wanted or needed and no matter how much I tried, I could not read her muddled mind. And then, my grief was huge when her doctor told me she had to be admitted to the nursing home. In hindsight, I know that I was ripe for post-traumatic stress or anxiety disorder. Most caregivers face elevated risk to their physical and mental health as well as to their finances and retirement. I have expressed to many friends that it took me about a year to begin to feel like myself again. As I look back, I think I was almost to the breaking point physically because of sheer exhaustion. When Mother was no longer living in my home, I experienced the empty nest syndrome which my friends have had when their children went away to college. Mother's return visits, however, were not joyful for either of us. She seemed to never remember having lived here and always begged to go home. I wrote in detail about that in another passage entitled "HOME." My greatest grief came when Mother no longer knew me or recognized me. She asked for *Bonnie* constantly but did not know me when she saw me. Mother's actual physical death was easier for me than her not knowing me as her daughter.

Other caregivers have told me about some of the fixations their patients have and a very common one seems to be ladies' purses. That was certainly true with my mother. Her fixation was so strong and her anxiety so great that I even had an identical purse on hand just in case the other one was put away so well that none of us could find it! After her illness progressed for a couple of years, she would put things in very illogical places. Some places that we found her purse were—under the sofa cushions, in the laundry hamper, in many different drawers, in the refrigerator—just to name a few. As soon as the purse was located Mother would put it down and a half-minute later ask, *Where's my purse?* And the search was on again.

Mother drove much longer that I thought she should. I knew that being able to drive was one of the final vestiges of independence and I delayed that decision to disable her vehicle way beyond the time it should have been done. Thank God for keeping her safe as well as all the other drivers she encountered. For as long as she was able to drive herself to town she would buy exactly the same things each trip—bananas, a chuck roast and toilet tissues. I did not have to purchase roast or toilet tissue for over a year after she went into the nursing home! She left me quite a stockpile.

It never mattered that she would have a shopping list. She would come home with her three items and tell me that the grocery store was out of everything on the list. If I were shopping with her, the only items she would put in her shopping cart were bananas, a chuck roast, and toilet tissue. All other items had to be placed in my cart. I think that when medical professionals and scientists truly understand Alzheimer's, if they ever do, that one of the world's greatest mysteries will have been solved. It is a very vicious disease that robs its victims of ordinary life and pleasures as they have known them. The professional caregivers of Alzheimer's patients are truly cut from a different and extremely special cloth. I thank each of them for taking care of very special patients. God will surely bless those caregivers.

For months before Mother went to live in the nursing home, I often thought I must be getting her disease because I could not keep knives in the kitchen! My kitchen is very well equipped since cooks shop for cooking utensils just as clothes horses shop for new fashions. Good sharp knives are absolutely necessary in food preparation but I had to resort to slicing a tomato with a steak knife more than once! I would casually mention to Mother that some of my knives were missing and she would become very defensive and tell me she had not seen *any* knives. The defensive posture is a common reaction of Alzheimer's patients; very much like that of a child who has been discovered doing something they know they shouldn't be doing. When Mother displayed that sort of behavior, it was useless to pursue it any further. And I would again, wonder if I was *catching* her disease. After Mother went to the nursing home, my maid and I started cleaning her *play house*, which is an apartment in the barn—a large kitchen/dining/sitting area with one bedroom and a handicapped bathroom and laundry room which Mother was able to leave as *messy* as she wanted. Her apartment in the main house was kept much neater. When we began cleaning out drawers in her play house, we kept finding knives. They were tucked in some strange places—one was even under the pillow in her cat's cradle! We found all sorts of things in the oddest places. After all the cleaning and sorting was done, we found thirty-nine knives in the barn! Remember, fixations of Alzheimer's patients vary greatly—these are just a few of my mother's. I'm sure other caregivers have similar tales to tell.

Fortunately, for all of us, my mother was passively pleasant most of the time. Many children of Alzheimer's patients have to deal with complete personality changes in their parents and all are not as blessed as I was. Mother had an innately sweet disposition and maintained that throughout much of her illness.

Mother's inability to function or live alone lasted a bit over ten years. The nursing home staff took such excellent care of her. They became *her family* and treated her as they would have treated their own mothers. I am truly grateful to all of them for their kindnesses and love they gave my mother and me.

There were many times when Mother provided entertainment for all of us. She was very small and physically agile. The geri-chairs are built well enough to safe keep almost any contortionist in its seat but not *Miss Margaret*, my mother. She could slide through the openings, never turn the chair over and surprise the nurses by setting off her ankle alarm as she started to leave her hall.

Mother never drank milk or ate any dairy products other than ice cream. Tomatoes—in any form—paste, sliced, stewed or in sauces would not pass her lips. That is, until she forgot that she didn't like them. This has always amazed me that her taste changed, or was it forgotten?

One day the head nurse on her hall called to ask me to come to see if I could help calm her. My mother was always the lady, very kind and sweet, soft spoken with a comforting nature. But something changed. She was swearing like a sailor and using words I had never heard. When I arrived at the security entrance to her hall, I could hear Mother's voice as soon as I entered the area. Her room was full of nurses, aides, and housekeepers whose mouths were agape. They were in total shock at Mother's salty language. As soon as I walked in the door (this was a good day and she recognized me) she invited me in with her sweetest, kindest motherly tone. I stayed for an hour or so before signaling to her primary nurse to distract Mother's attention so that I could leave. As soon as I was out of her sight, she began her tirade again. This went on for several hours but once she had a good night's sleep, she never cursed again.

Mother was such a *busy bee* that the nurses on her hall took care of other patients with Mother in tow. She loved to work and they were so good to give her little jobs to entertain her (and to try to keep her out of trouble)! Mother probably came as close as any patient can to having one on one care. Because they loved her so, her caregivers put forth the effort it took to keep her from *failing nursing home.*

Probably my most angst-filled time with Mother was when I became afraid that she was *failing* nursing home. She never knew which room was hers and, therefore, thought all of them were hers. And their contents were hers as well. So when she was rambling around, she would go into other patient's rooms, rummage through their closets, etc. and claim any item she liked. On one of those afternoons, she encountered a patient who was together enough mentally to recognize that Mother had taken a scarf from her drawer. A tug of war ensued and Mother, who had great upper body strength for a small person, punched the lady and made her fall. For a few hours, until the x-rays were read, it was feared that Mother's *opponent* had a broken hip. But we were spared. Her hip was not broken. Mother was treated for a urinary tract infection which justified her aggressive behavior. Thank God for preventing her from *failing nursing home.*

I was the youngest of three girls. My half-sister was seven years older than I and my sister was three and a half years older than I. While making small talk with Mother, after she went to live in the nursing home, she told me she had *four* children. This came as such a shock to me and she was unable to tell me anything more about that fourth child. Few of her friends were still living by that time but fortunately, one of them was able to fill in the gaps for me. Mother had miscarried a three month pregnancy, a baby boy, which she had always wanted, while I was in the hospital with polio. Her friend was able to tell me that this was such a great loss to Mother and much of what I had thought was depression resulting from my having polio was related to losing this baby. I thought I knew my Mother's every secret but this was one she never shared until she was no longer able to fill in the blanks.

A son would have been such a blessing to Mother. She was multi-talented and did everything well. She loved to garden, both flower and vegetable. Fishing was one of the few things Mother and Daddy enjoyed together. She was a farmer—of cows, hogs, corn and pastures. A son would have been a wonderful helpmate to her. In the evenings after her bath and dinner, she was always sewing some project. She crocheted, did beautiful embroidery, made almost all our clothes—evening gowns and wedding dresses, and quilted with a passion.

It was so sad to see her lose the ability to concentrate long enough to do any of the things she had always enjoyed. But in her mind, she still thought she was doing all of them. And baking the world's best pound cakes, too!

I encourage you, if given the task of caregiving, to realize that none of us can give one-hundred-percent of ourselves without feeling tired, sad, impatient or even angry. I hope that you will determine your priorities while acknowledging your limitations. Limitations come from simply being human, not damaged or incompetent.

# TRUST

Trust is a kind of gift. We give it to others in the hope that they will not abuse it. We put our faith in our spouses, doctors and friends and believe they will honor our hearts and our health as we honor theirs. One of the saddest moments in my life was seeing my mother lose all trust and security when two men came to our home on Saturday night, August 15, 1998. She seemed to be coming down with a summer cold and was not feeling well. I gave her some cold medicine and put her to bed about 8:30 p.m. After she was settled in, I got ready for bed and went upstairs to work until I got sleepy. The medication I gave mother should have helped her get some much needed rest and I was sure she would sleep soundly. I usually work in total silence or with easy listening music but on this particular night I had the TV on a special program I wanted to see. As is my habit, I was working with great concentration. Lady D, my beautiful obedient, tri-colored collie had barked a couple of times but I interpreted her bark as an alarm for last call outside. I told her I'd be down in a few minutes to take her to potty. She was one of the few dogs I've ever known who would not traverse the stairs—ever. So she obediently sat at the bottom of the stairs. After another two or three minutes she barked again, this time a bit more aggressively to tell me to come downstairs—now. At almost the same moment, at approximately ten o'clock, I heard Mother at the base of the stairs calling up to me. Her dementia was advanced to the point that she was usually disoriented upon waking. I attributed her strange remarks to her condition. She was telling me that someone was at the back door asking to be let in. When I got halfway down the stairs, I could see the sheer fright in her eyes and realized that there must be people outside. I was attempting to calm Mother but to no avail. For the first time since I had come to live in this house, I felt very uncomfortable; so much so that I picked up my loaded 38 caliber pistol as we came through the bedroom. Since there were more lights on outside than inside, I was able to see that there was an unfamiliar van in the back yard. It was parked so that my and Mother's vehicles were blocked in.

When I got to the door I asked, "Who's there?"

No reply.

"Who's out there?"

No answer.

Then more deeply—"What do you want?"

And still, no reply.

Finally, I asked, "Who are you?"

A very gruff voice answered, "Junior". Junior was a very nice young man who had worked for me in the afternoons after school, on Saturdays, and full time during the summer. He had stopped working a couple of weeks earlier so he could prepare himself for college classes which would begin in September. He was very polite and was so soft spoken that I sometimes had to lip read to hear him. I knew immediately that the gruff voice I had just heard was not Junior, but someone pretending to be him. I went along with this stranger and let him think he had fooled me. I began talking to him through the door. He told me that he wanted to talk to me about his uncle Mitch but needed to come inside, out of hearing of Mitch who was supposedly with him.

Mitchell Gregory had worked for me for years but I had to let him go when his drug use and problems therewith became obvious. He is completely recovered from his addictions and I have since rehired him. Mitch was and still is one of the finest men I know and is physically the strongest man I've ever known. Mitch is from a large family of exceptionally talented people. He had introduced me to his nephew, Junior, and I was pleased to have this young man work for me.

Again, I was going along with whatever the person outside my door said. I told him that he knew not to come to my home after dark and that if he wanted to talk to me, he'd have to do so on the telephone. I told him to "leave; leave right now". Mother and I walked into my kitchen to watch him leave. The young man who boarded that van was certainly not Junior. He was tall, thin, had his hair in corn rows and was someone I had never seen. He slowly got into the passenger side of a dark blue, older model van. The driver was in no hurry to leave. After a few minutes, the van, with lights off, backed into a new rose bed near the barn. They drove down the drive and stopped again, very near the fountain. Mother and I were easing through the almost dark house and watching them in the fairly-well lit yard. Soon—a few moments later—the van drove across the front lawn and parked parallel to the highway. They sat there for several minutes as Mother and I watched from the living room windows. A car went along the highway and we were able to get a very good look at the van. The van sped away as soon as that car passed so Mother and I breathed sighs of relief that they were finally gone.

I turned my attention to Mother and tried calming her as we headed to the kitchen for some milk and cookies. As we left the foyer and entered my bedroom, I heard glass breaking at the back door. With gun still in hand, I approached the door and told the person outside that I had a gun and would use it if he did not leave. He hit the leaded glass door again, very near the door knob and the welds in the stained glass gave slightly but did not break completely. Had it given way, the perpetrator would have been able to reach inside and open the door. I finally allowed myself to realize the grave danger Mother and I were facing and picked up the phone to call 911. After dialing the numbers, I put the phone to my ear. There was a totally deafening silence which made me know that the phone lines had been cut.

At that very moment, I became aware that we were going to die. The smell of death hung so heavily around me that I could taste it. Death, to me, smelled and tasted like hot, dirty, smelly money—like coins and bills held tightly in one's sweaty hands while in line at the beach, on a boiling hot day, waiting to buy an icee. For many months after this threat to our lives, I could with no effort, still smell and taste that nastiness. When called on to give depositions, testify or recount the events of that life changing night, I was encased by that horrible stench.

Everything I did from this point forward was under the direction of a Higher Power. As I placed the phone back on the receiver, I saw two figures crouching beneath my kitchen windows. In hindsight, I know that I should have shot them both. Lady D was barking and throwing herself against those windows. I was so afraid she would be hurt if she broke through the glass. For the first time in my life, the only time in my life, I know what parents must feel like when protecting their children. My Mother and Lady D were <u>my</u> <u>children</u>.

My bedroom is completely surrounded by other rooms and can be easily closed off from the rest of the house. As I closed the door to the kitchen and the door to the laundry/bath area I was repeatedly asking Mother to sit on the bed until I came back to her. Her dementia had shortened her attention span to almost none. As I reached for the doorknob to close off the foyer, Lady D threw herself against that door, opening it all the way and ran, barking loudly around the corner to the whirlpool bath. Shards of glass were falling to the floor and into the bathtub. I placed my left hand on Lady D's head and shot where I had seen movement of the curtain. Again, all at once, everything was silent. In a few seconds, I lifted the window dressing on the door to see if there was a dead man on the ground outside. I had obviously missed. But, as if to say "I'll kill you", I shot again through the hole in the window of the door.

By this time I was determined that this person(s) had to be caught and punished for their actions. I quickly slipped on jeans and a shirt, all the while telling Mother to stay inside while I went across the highway to my neighbor's to call for help. My bag cell phone was in my car in the back yard and I could not gather the strength to go where I had seen those two men lurking. But, as I left the safety I had felt in my home, I expected to be attacked when I went out the door. My mind was racing as I went across the front yard, gun still in hand. When I got to the highway, which is usually a fairly busy thoroughfare, I looked to the west and there was no car in sight. As I looked, east, toward Troy, there was the van which had been in my back yard earlier that evening! Its lights were on and the engine was running. At this point my primary fear was that they would speed toward me and run me over. The highway is only about sixteen feet wide, but it seemed to take me forever to get to the other side. My mind was filled with many racing thoughts. If my husband Rex had sent them to kill me, he would surely have told them that I am a very determined person. Since their attempted entry had failed, they might be waiting for me to go for help. My logical mind was telling me that if they sped toward me that the heavy concrete culvert at my neighbor's driveway might stop them. I ran to get to his porch, knocked on his door and he answered almost immediately. I told him to notice the parked van and began telling him to call for help. After I recounted some of the events of the night to him, he was in total shock. Finally, I asked him if I was talking so fast that he couldn't hear me. At that moment, we saw two men jump down a steep embankment and run toward the van on the passenger side. My neighbor telephoned 911 to post an APB for the three people, possibly four, in an older model dark blue van. As the van left its parking spot, it headed towards the west, toward Luverne and the driver hit the brakes briefly as though he might be picking up someone else at the end of my property. The driver, the two men who boarded on the passenger's side and that other man, if there was one at the end of my property, would have brought the count to four. The Luverne police stopped the van when it reached Luverne but since there were only two people on board they allowed them to go on their merry way. "Barney Phyfe" must have been on duty that night! It is approximately ten miles from my house to Luverne so several people could have vacated that van along the way. Evidently, no consideration was given to that fact.

In court testimony, after the fact, I learned that when I shot at the men who were trying to break into my home, the one who had the 25 caliber pistol jumped down from my retaining wall and dropped the gun under some shrubbery. They were criminally experienced enough to know that they could never leave behind that kind of hard evidence. One of the men stated that they were looking for the gun by the light of a cigarette lighter when they heard voices across the highway. They had no idea that one of those voices was mine asking my neighbor to call for help. The fact that they were distracted by the gun search gave me the opportunity to get to my neighbor's door. I shudder to think what the outcome could have been if they had actually been waiting for me to come outside.

We are very fortunate to live in a county which can boast about its very efficient and effective law enforcement team. Within minutes after my neighbor's call for help, we had two deputies and an investigator on the scene. After relating to them what had happened one of the deputies told me how fortunate I was to still be alive. By this time, I was reasoning on my own again and knew that this was true.

The investigator was able to splice my phone lines back together and my first call was to my attorney, Tony King at one o'clock in the morning. His immediate reaction was that Rex had sent these men. His reaction was justifiable in light of the fact that Rex had forced Mr. King's car off the highway a couple of weeks earlier. My attorney actually felt that he had been stalked by Rex. He had a lovely wife and two young sons. There were many times when I feared that he would not continue to represent me because of Rex's craziness.

When you have loved and trusted someone as I had Rex, it is impossible to comprehend that they could betray you in such a violent manner. The consensus of opinion pointed this vicious attack to Rex but I would not allow myself to believe this could be true.

Mother and I were so shaken that we awaited daylight as anxious children await Santa Claus. When morning finally broke, we were amazed to see how much damage had actually been done to our property. The back steps were covered with glass which had comprised the sheet of obscure glass which was on the outside of the leaded glass at the back door. This door was damaged beyond repair and had to be replaced entirely. The three phone lines, one to the main house, one to Mother's apartment and the fax and internet line to the studio had all been cut completely and partially torn out of the box. The door to the whirlpool bath was able to be repaired by replacing the upper glass portion and repainting the rest. The security light at the whirlpool bath door had been broken and an attempt had been made to pull it out of the wall. Obviously, these men were determined to gain entry into our home.

Living in small town, USA, is a wonderful experience. Friends and neighbors flocked in on Sunday, bringing food, cheer and curiosity. Some of them brought tools to temporarily repair damages. Others came with additional motion sensor lights to install that very day. My dear friend and protector, Carter Sanders, came with shotgun in hand and spent Sunday night with us, just in case these idiots decided to return. Mother and I were so exhausted by Sunday night that we could have slept standing up. Thank God we had Carter standing guard for us!

Carter had come to spend the night on another occasion. When Rex decided he needed to go on a trip to an undisclosed destination, Carter felt that we needed to be sure he had actually gone on a trip and that he would not come back unexpectedly to harm me. At the time of his departure, I had no idea where he was going; only later did my instincts point to Mexico. (More on that trip in Mexico! Oh Mexico!).

Monday morning, about 10 a.m., I was shown several photos of older model vans, dark in color. One in particular stood out. I was able to identify it from all angles. Since I make my living as an artist and live in a visual world, I can with great certainty give you minute details regarding almost any and everything I see. Until this very day, I do not know the make or model of that van (Ford, Chevy, etc.) but could identify it in a lineup of hundreds of vans.

At noon on Monday I received a call from Sheriff Russell Thomas telling me that one of the men had turned himself in at the Luverne Police Department. When he arrived there he was driving that same dark blue van and asked if the police were looking for him. Pike County Sheriff's Department had issued an arrest warrant for him, sent it over to Luverne and yes, they were ready to pick him up. When they searched the van they found a 25 caliber pistol as well as several rounds of ammunition. They also learned that the driver's side door would not open. It now became clear why the men always boarded on the passenger's side.

Bubba Dixon, a 40 year old black male was arrested and sent to Pike County jail. He stated that he was safer in jail than on the street. And he immediately told who his accomplice had been. From that point forward, everything else he said was basically false. I was able to hear much of his interview through closed circuit television in the Sheriff's office. I spent the afternoon at the Pike County Courthouse and was able to hear the lies and foul language of Demetrius DeShon Oliver, aka "Meathead" as he was brought in and placed in custody of the Sheriff's Department. I had never heard anyone talk like this being. The words he used to describe me, a total and complete stranger to him, are too vulgar to be written by my pen. I had never seen this person prior to Saturday night when he boarded that van in my backyard. He told that he had worked for me and that I owed him money for that labor. He very convincingly stated that he had come to my house to collect the money which was due him. I was awed by his demeanor. All of this was a first for me. An old remark that "the truth was not in him" could not be truer.

By Monday night, some of our sheriff's deputies and investigators had gone for nearly sixty hours with no sleep. Dedication to job and justice like this is hard to find. I am very grateful to them for removing these two villains from the streets, even for a short time.

The protection that was afforded my mother and me on that night came from my Heavenly Father. Even though their scheme was very well planned, they were actually powerless and confused in their effort to harm us.

Mother and I had to begin recovery from this horrifying event. For weeks, even months thereafter, this permeated every aspect of our lives. The inconveniences we experienced were numerous but the one I think everyone can best identify with is the one regarding bathing. I have for many years enjoyed the luxury and therapy of a whirlpool bath. The jets are noisy even on the lowest setting. While in the shower, we are inundated with the sound of spraying water. Either type of bath is a wonderful retreat from the doorbell, ringing phone and general stresses of living. For many months after this experience, I had to bathe during daylight hours. If time did not permit my bath during the day, I had to wait until the next morning to bathe. I remember, very vividly, when God gave me relief from this. If I had to go outside after dark, even with lots of lights on, I was constantly looking over my shoulder, so much so that the tension in my neck was extreme. At dusk dark, on a Sunday evening, I had to refill my dog's food canister from the battery house in the backyard. When I stepped off the bottom step onto the grass, I suddenly was not afraid. There was a glorious peace that came over me. Those months of constant fear and dread were finally over. I actually felt like a heavy fog around me had suddenly lifted and I could see clearly now. My Mother never regained that security and I shall always regret that. Her Alzheimer's was advanced enough that she was not able to realize that the likelihood of a repeated affront was remote. When she no longer knew or recognized me as her daughter, she could in fair detail tell of that night's frightening experience.

The younger man, 21 year old Demetrius Oliver, was the man I saw board the dark colored van, passenger's side door, in my back yard. In the light provided by the outside security lamps I saw that his reddish brown hair was in plaits and that his skin was not extremely dark. He was thin and tall and young. His gruff voice betrayed his youth and was the one who tried to talk me into opening the door to him. By their own testimony, the two villains admitted that the older man, Bubba Dixon, was standing on the top step, back against the outside wall, holding the 25 caliber pistol up in the air and waiting for me to open the door. He had told the younger man to talk us into opening the door and he could go back to the van. He had told him that he *would take care of both of us*. I truly believe that had they gained entrance, neither my mother nor I would have seen the light of day on that Sunday morning or any day thereafter.

Since I was certain I could identify Demetrius Oliver, I was ready to go to trial. When I entered the courtroom, I was surprised to see a clean shaven head and face on a well-dressed young man whose shirt was tucked into tailored pants. There was no doubt in my mind that this complete transformation was for the benefit of the judge and jury but was wasted on me. His deliberate constant stare at me was unnerving and intimidating. This was obviously not his first visit to a courtroom.

His mother's testimony amazed me when she, under oath, told what a good boy he was and that he had never been in trouble before. She completely forgot to say that he had a bullet still in his arm which he had gotten when he tried to rob a small gas station six months earlier. According to Alabama law, that bullet must be causing a life threatening infection or he must give permission for the surgical removal of it, before it can be tested to prove it came from the gun which was fired by that store owner. The jury had difficulty understanding why Mr. Oliver was charged with burglary, third degree, rather than attempted murder. I too have always questioned the wisdom of the District Attorney's office in allowing that to be the charge. I have been told that they felt they were sure they could get a conviction on the burglary charge. By the time the jury returned to the courtroom with their guilty verdict, there was standing room only. The judge gave him the maximum sentence of 20 years. I was delighted to hear that verdict but was soon to learn that his incarceration would be much less than that. The time he had already served while awaiting trial as well as the 75 days off sentence for each thirty days served meant that he would actually serve less than six years.

In my feeble attempt to insure his maximum time in prison I wrote to every congressman, senator and appropriate official to request that

I be allowed to attend any and all parole board hearings regarding this individual. I, from time to time, called the local parole officials to remind them of my written request. This turned out to be one of those situations in which the *squeaky wheel was certainly not greased.* My concerted attention to detail was completely ignored.

But, the crowning glory of this entire fiasco was that the renowned, inefficient, overpaid and incapable Alabama Parole Board released this individual because some clerk in that office flagged his file as a *victimless crime*! I shall defy any and every one until my dying day that my mother and I were victims. This was truly a life changing event for me and traumatized my mother beyond repair.

The State of Alabama needs to completely revamp its Prison Commission and pay a lot more attention to protecting the innocent rather than the guilty! A review board comprised of people who have been violated by criminal perpetrators as well as the prison system should be appointed to monitor the conditions whereby each criminal gains release. Those who have been affected as my mother and I were could contribute much to the system which is apparently very broken.

Bubba Dixon, the forty year old perpetrator was granted a plea bargain and sentenced to approximately 4 ½ years prison time. I had no choice but to accept this because I did not see his face that horrible night and if I had been asked if I had seen him at my home on August 15, 1998, I would have had to say, "No". Nor did I hear his voice. I have learned more facts about our justice system than I ever wanted to know. One of those is that for every thirty days served, seventy five days is taken off one's sentence. The time one is held in jail prior to trial also counts as time served, using that same formula. If for instance, he received a sentence of 4 ½ years and served approximately nine months before trial date, he would actually serve only twelve months, more or less, in prison. These are approximations, of course. During Bubba's time in prison, he was allowed work release privileges until someone told me they had seen him in Luverne, on a weekend, buying beer at a convenience store. After the violence my mother and I had experienced, I became livid upon learning this and began a campaign to keep him from having these privileges. I wrote to every congressman, senator, parole office, and law enforcement group I could imagine. Needless to say, his privileges were revoked and he actually became a prisoner for the rest of his jail time.

In order for you, the reader, to realize how very serious this entire situation could have been, I must add this footnote:

Soon after Bubba Dixon was released from prison he became involved with a woman who had a twenty-one year old daughter. He lived with them and one night, while that mother was at work, he raped and sodomized that young girl and then loaded her into that same dark blue van. He took her to the Rutledge Bridge, drove to the water's edge and raped and sodomized her with a roofing hammer. He put her back in the van and drove her to a deserted shack in a wooded area in south Crenshaw County. He then tied her feet and hands together with an extension cord and threw an old blanket over her, leaving her for dead.

The next day, she heard logging trucks and chain saws in the area. She crawled through the woods approximately one half mile and was able to flag down a logging truck. The driver, when he approached her, was told, "Bubba Dixon did this to me" before she lost consciousness, again. Because of the serious injuries she had sustained and excessive blood loss, it was at first doubtful that she would live. She did, however, survive.

When officers went to the house he shared with her and her mother, Bubba Dixon stated to police that he thought she was dead. He was taken straight to jail.

# THE FOOL IN ME

The fool in me loves too much, trusts too much and talks too much. I also feel too much, take too many chances, win sometimes and lose often. On occasion, I lack self-control. Laughter, for me, can be totally uncontrolled—so much so that I lose my breath and can't utter an audible sound. If I get the giggles my family and friends know to give me a few minutes to "get over it". If I become really tired or frustrated, I get a laughing spell rather than becoming angry and/or lashing out at those around me. I call this the fool in me for lack of a better description.

Almost everything I do, I do to the extreme. I've always recognized that I have tremendous weakness and have therefore avoided most things that lead to addictions. I have always been a workaholic. This behavior is usually socially accepted but it can be just as serious a malady as any. It has, in the past created strife in relationships. Others have told me that I am too driven. The perfectionist in me probably would have consumed me totally had it not been for the fool in me.

# RESILIENCE

Resilient people are like trees bending in the wind. They bounce back. Highly resilient people do not fall apart—at least not for long. They call on their inner strength and keep moving forward. Some common qualities are shared by resilient people and can be learned. Relying on others helps them through tough times. Having a positive attitude is always an asset.

Worry, per se, is a waste of energy. Take appropriate action to correct a situation over which you have control. Dismiss those situations over which you have none. Asking for help, seeking resources, learning new skills and changing your path are things resilient people do. When we gain strength from adversity and convert misfortune into blessings we become better people. Difficulties should be considered temporary. Expect to overcome them. It is never *if* tribulation comes, but *when*. Troubles will come to all of us.

Evil exists because people make poor choices. Even though we cannot control the crises in our lives, we can be constructive in our responses to them. We have the choice of *going* through or *growing* through them.

Believing that *everything that happens, happens for the best* has brought me through some very difficult times. My faith in God continues to see me through all things. I know that wherever the trouble comes from that it has passed through His hand before arriving at my door.

In 1954, one year before the Salk vaccine was developed, I was diagnosed with polio. I was, for years, very limited as to physical activities. Since I was house bound and spent much time in bed, I had to entertain myself with quiet work and play. Once I learned to love reading, I was never lonely. The characters in books entertained me and I was able to travel broadly, experience very exciting people and places and learn about things to which children my age normally never gave a moment's thought. I learned to knit, crochet, embroider and sew at a very early age. My parents provided hoops, threads, special needles, and instruction booklets. I still contend that if you gave me the instructions for building a rocket I could do it—just give me some guidance and I'm on my way. Since my parents were certainly not wealthy, I had to improvise on many levels and for that I am most grateful. My creative spirit blossomed early and is still in high gear. Friends and family often state that I can take almost nothing and create something beautiful from it. Because of the many avenues opened for me, I consider having had polio an asset; it was certainly not a handicap.

Since I was on crutches for years, I had the privilege of having the boys in my class carry my books and open doors for me. I grew accustomed to being treated like a lady and my husband almost always opens my car door and makes sure I'm comfortably seated. I find myself expecting the things to which I grew accustomed early in life.

The fact that I was predicted never to walk again did not hinder me. I knew I would walk and after many years of physical therapy I walk with barely a limp. If I am really tired, I have to be careful about traversing steps and stairs. Other than that, normal activities are enjoyed on a daily basis. I have geared my life so that activities which would present problems for me are simply not a part of my life or interest. This lemon has become my lemonade.

PPS or post-polio syndrome is something I really thought I would escape. Apparently, I have not been spared. For those of us who had the disease when we were young are being re-visited. This time, however, our resilience is not nearly as great as it was in our youth. A few months ago, a muscle in the calf of my right leg contracted and no matter what I did to relax it, nothing worked. Prolonged contraction of muscles causes atrophy and this is a very common complaint of polio victims. I also have a muscle in my lower right arm that appears to be acting up as well. I will attempt to keep my positive outlook and know that God wants me to change directions—again. I hope to be able to continue to write and if that is what God wants me to do, prepare to read many more of my memoirs.

# FINANCIAL BLESSINGS ABOUND

Credit scores dictate many decisions in our lives; both that we make and that others make for us. After living in an apartment for a while, I knew that I must have a house so I began the search in the midst of the very difficult divorce from Rex. He had been my personal banker for thirteen years before we were married and I had trusted him with my everything. All that we owned, except our house which had been built on property which had been homesteaded into my family, was in <u>his</u> name alone, even my personal car and my life insurance. I was never concerned about that because I had trusted him implicitly. It had never occurred to me that I had no banking relationships until I found the house at Rural Home which I wanted to buy. I telephoned the two local banks and each of their loan officers asked for my social security number only.

The local Seminole Bank had its own board of directors but larger loans had to have the approval of a special loan committee. I was told, after the fact, that when the local bank representative went to that loan committee meeting in the afternoon after I made my request that he had three applications to present. He presented the other two because he felt they had a good chance for approval. He then presented mine and when telling the committee members about my request, one of the members of that loan committee listened intently and asked my name. When he identified me the gentleman said to let me have the loan. He had lost a family member and I had created artwork for him from those funeral flowers. My work has created far reaching relationships for me and for that, I will be forever grateful.

Remember that I was a "starving artist", unemployed for all practical purposes and had been a housewife for twenty plus years. I never filled out a loan application or provided a financial statement or verification of income to either bank. Both banks telephoned me the next morning to say they would loan me the money I needed. One of them offered a slightly less interest rate so I opted to have them provide my mortgage loan. I did not realize at that time what a miracle, what a true blessing I had just received. As I look back to that time, I am still awed by how this loan was granted.

From the moment I decided, finally, to leave Rex, it has been as though God, blesses all that I do. When I have shared the circumstances surrounding my buying this lovely old home to people who hold enviable financial positions in our society, they, too, have been shocked that no red tape was required.

Larger financial institutions have many safeguards in place to enforce their system of checks and balances. Every *i* must be dotted and every *t* must be crossed before a penny is loaned, generally. However, about three years ago, I received a call from a loan officer at one of America's largest lending institutions offering to refinance my mortgage so I could continue to have the interest deduction for income tax purposes. I was working in my studio that rainy afternoon and had not even considered such a thing as refinancing my loan. I told her I didn't have the time nor did I want to provide a bunch of paperwork to her but if she could give me some basic information regarding interest rate, payment amounts, etc. that I would look at them. Several weeks earlier, I had discarded a solicitation from that same bank without even reading it. This industrious young woman was making follow-up calls and we connected immediately. She called the following morning with the particular details I had requested, including a very favorable interest rate, and told me the only thing I would need was a new appraisal. I had made some major renovations, done extensive landscaping and added an apartment to accommodate my mother. I was anxious to see how much value had been added as a result of much *sweat equity.* The banker was able to arrange for an appraiser to come out a couple of days later and when we received her appraisal, we were delighted to know how much the property had appreciated. Again, I was granted a large loan with no proof of income or paperwork of any kind. I am the only person I know who has received these large loan amounts with such ease.

*Luck* is being in the right place at the right time but blessings truly abound. Many times in my life I have wanted to rush matters to conclusion only to learn later, sometimes much much later, that the delays were for my benefit. The following accounts provide amazing proof that everything happens for the best.

Sun Bank, Rex's employer, provided excellent health insurance for its employees and their families. When I decided to leave Rex my concerns were far greater than health insurance. I continued to be covered under his plan until the divorce was final and then was allowed COBRA coverage for an additional year. Most insurance companies will not even take the application of polio survivors because all too often, it revisits those people fifteen to forty years later. Since we are really among the first generation of survivors, the protocol for treatment has not been established. The outcome of post polio syndrome is, more often than not, not a pretty sight. Because of my medical history, I was considered uninsurable as an individual. My physician suggested I contact the State of Alabama Insurance Commission to investigate a new program which was being established to provide health insurance for the people who were considered uninsurable by industry standards because of past medical conditions and/or self-employment and not belonging to an insurable group. I prayed daily for this whole divorce fiasco to be over but Rex began representing himself in the courtroom. I'm still not sure if he fired his attorney or if the attorney had 'fired' him. Due to his inadequacies and delay tactics, the State had time to open this new insurance program on June 1, 1999. My COBRA coverage ended midnight May 31, 1999. Is this amazing or what? God's delays are not denials! I had no lapse in coverage and counted my blessings daily. Below is the article introducing the new state health plan;

# State to implement health insurance plan

ASSOCIATED PRESS

Alabamians who lose group health insurance may soon be able to get coverage through a state-run program, but it won't come cheap.

State insurance officials say coverage through the Alabama Health Plan could cost up to twice as much as standard insurance policies. But the state program won't reject people because of health problems.

The plan, which will not cover everyone who needs insurance, is Alabama's answer to new federal laws designed to keep people from forfeiting health coverage when they lose or change jobs. State Insurance Commissioner Mickey DeBellis said he approved the plan Wednesday after receiving no objections in a hearing on the proposal.

DeBellis said he hopes to have the program available by Jan. 1.

Insurance interests helped draft the plan and consider it the best approach to meet federal mandates. But some expressed concerns about what the program will cost taxpayers and how it will affect insurance costs overall.

"It's a well-intended piece of (federal) legislation that is going to have a dramatic impact on the cost of overall health care," said Byron McCain, executive director of the Alabama Association of Health Maintenance Organizations.

He said many of the people in the pool will probably be bad insurance risks, with existing health problems and medical expenses exceeding their premium payments.

"It's tragic that people lose their health insurance, but I'm not sure that we're going to make overall health insurance more available," he said. State taxpayers will eventually pay the price if, as expected, premiums don't pay the medical expenses of those in the plan. Companies that provide standard health insurance will divvy up the amount needed by the state health insurance program and then receive a dollar-for-dollar tax credit for that expense, said Ralph R. Norman III, a lawyer for the state Insurance Department.

The state is uncertain how many people will apply for insurance in the program, he said. Similar pools in Louisiana and Mississippi covered between 500 and 800 people in 1995, while Tennessee's at one point topped 3,000 in recent years, Norman said.

To get in the plan, people must have had 18 months of continuous coverage in a group health plan. But they can't be eligible any longer for group coverage, or for Medicaid or Medicare.

Even though this insurance was very expensive, I at least had health insurance! And then, when Gene and I were married on December 12, 2005, I became eligible for Tricare, the wonderful insurance provided to military retirees and their dependents. And now that I am 65 plus, I have Medicare coverage as well. The health issues we currently have are handled by very competent physicians, therapists and facilities and are paid in full. If all goes well and our government does not completely ruin health care for our entire nation, we should continue to be covered.

Since I had worked outside the home for only a few years of my life, I decided to wait until age 65 to start drawing my social security benefits. Some little voice inside me kept telling me to go to the Social Security office in Montgomery to make application for those benefits. My husband and I drove up and planned the entire day to sit and wait to be seen by a government employee. We were fortunate to have only a short waiting period before we were called back to meet with a very polite, nice young woman. She was very efficient and answered all my questions regarding my benefits based on my earnings and those of my ex-husband. We were ready to leave her office when she asked if I had been married to anyone other than Gene, my current husband, and Rex, my ex-husband. I had been married to C. Allen Blackstock (see chapter entitled, ALLEN) for

13 years, from 1965 to 1978. He died about a couple of years after we were divorced. I had delayed marrying my present husband only because of a very busy schedule until December 12, 2005. Little did I know that had I married him 9 months earlier, I would not have reached my 61st birthday (which was the primary criteria) for my being able to draw social security benefits based on my first husband's earnings. Because of a few little publicized or known facts, I was granted an additional $600.00 per month income from social security. Wonders never cease in my life! There is no way I could plan these delays, dates, and deeds to my benefit but God certainly takes care of the details for me! My blessings continue to be exceedingly abundant, above and beyond what I can ever deserve.

# STAMPED UPON MY HEART

When I was young, I loved to take a quilt or blanket, spread it on the grass, and watch the clouds form all sorts of images. My husband and I continue to share this pleasure any time we're outside or driving.

If there were no clouds, I would lie on the grass, staring into space and trace my place in the huge scheme of things: first name, last name, address, state, country, continent and universe. Starting with myself, I could gradually enlarge the loop until it encompassed everything. Or, I could shrink that loop until only I was still inside. This activity made me feel unique and at the same time connected. This exercise was, I think, the beginning of my thankfulness.

I am thankful for everything! Especially, for my husband who puts up with me from morn to night with tolerance, kindness and affection. I am thankful for the man he is—stable, mature, unselfish, intelligent, totally honest, caring and sweet.

I'm thankful for straightforward people who speak right up and tell it like it is, even if it is something that hits me squarely between the eyes and is not so pleasant. I much prefer this to sifting through nice comments to learn just how someone feels about an issue.

I'm thankful for energetic younger ones who remind me of my heyday when nothing was too much trouble or too difficult to undertake.

I'm thankful for my own contemporaries who have grey hair, wrinkles and slowing steps, who can't remember names and places.

I'm thankful I've learned the art of doing nothing. When I have felt overwhelmed, I realized that it was from trying to do and to be everything. I'm thankful I've learned to be still and quiet and wait for solutions and answers. I've learned that doubt means don't. Don't move. Don't answer. Don't move forward.

I'm thankful for learning to try and fail and try and fail again. Failure is a signpost to turn in another direction.

I'm thankful for learning that my thoughts are just thoughts; they are not necessarily truths. I'm glad I'm learning not to set unrealistically high standards for myself or for others.

I'm thankful I've learned that the world will not fall apart if I make a choice that goes against popular opinion. I'm thankful that I've learned that worrying is a waste of time. Actually, for me, it is a sin. God has never failed me and I don't believe he will do so today. I've learned to use that same energy I would have used worrying doing something about whatever was worrying me. If it is within my power to correct or rectify a situation, then I will take that action. If it is completely outside of my realm, then I will dismiss it. (I must admit that this lesson took me fifty plus years to learn but was well worth the wait)!

I'm thankful for finally learning that love doesn't hurt. It feels really good.

I'm glad I've learned that every day brings me a chance to start over. And I'm thankful for the hand of nature's perfection.

I'm thankful for learning that people who are always right, never get it. Those who cannot change their minds cannot change anything.

I'm thankful for having lived long enough to learn most of the rules, so I know which ones I can break.

I'm thankful that the Lord has been good in all directions and that my cup runneth over. I do not want to know if I am deserving—I only want the time, capacity and space to be forever grateful.

# CERTIFIED GENTLEMAN

Accidents, illnesses and traumatic events are of tremendous value to those who will accept them as indications that change is required—change in thoughts, attitudes and actions. Some are drawn closer to friends and family because we lose some of that haughty independence. If we listen to that small voice inside we realize what is really important—being free of pain, being clean and comfortable—just the basics—no frills—and what we receive from others—loving sacrifice and care.

When I broke my arm I was not heeding the warnings I was being given. On the morning of my accident, before I got out of bed, I asked God to help me get through a brunch I had scheduled for twenty-six members of a garden club from out of town. This was accomplished with style and grace. As soon as the excess food was stored and the kitchen cleaned, I had errands to run in town. I had also told God that I would rest that afternoon and possibly the next day. I wasn't getting to the rest part fast enough to suit Him so He put me down for a much longer time than I planned. On my first stop in town, at the local vet's office to pick up Lady D's medication refill, my foot slipped on some gravel as I stepped out of the car. I fell across a concrete walkway into the side of his building. The sudden stop yielded some very serious pain in my arm which would not move on its own. I never halfway do things—I do them very well or not at all. Same here—I broke my arm in two places. Since I took no medications and appeared to be in excellent health, the orthopedic doctor who saw me in the emergency room asked if I would like to heal naturally rather than with pins and rods. Realigning the broken bone without anesthesia pushed me over the edge with pain. An overnight stay in the hospital was necessary to get my pain to a manageable level. I came home about noon the next day and my friends took excellent care of me. On Saturday, my friend of 27 years came by to check on me. He was unaware that anything was wrong until he saw me. My lawn needed mowing and he said he'd never seen the grass so tall. My timing was not good—I had let my gardener go a week earlier. Gene Sykes told me not to worry about hiring someone else—that he would take care of my yard until I was back on my feet. He worked 6 days a week, long hours in the poultry industry and was still willing to give me his one day a week off—without pay. Gene had, for years, been the person I called when anything was broken, from tractor to mower to electrical appliances. The man is a genius and can fix anything. I had great respect for him and his abilities.

My recovery was coming right along but never fast enough for me. I had received a call to go to a local church to pick up some funeral flowers to preserve and as I was ready to go there, Gene was mowing the grass around the back door. I asked him if he would take a break and watch some food I had cooking. I needed it to be taken out of the oven in twenty minutes and knew that I would be gone longer than that. He was always willing to do anything I asked of him.

By the time I returned, he had lunch on the table and while waiting for the food to finish cooking, he'd heard the clothes dryer click off. I was still having to wear a sling. As I looked in on him, he was standing by my bed, folding the laundry which just happened to be my underwear. I was more than embarrassed but even more impressed that a man would actually be thoughtful enough to fold the laundry. As he said, it was much easier for him to fold the laundry with two hands than for me to do it with only one.

Gene and I were only friends—but because we were both alone, we began to have several meals a week together. It was just as easy to cook for two as for one. He offered to take me to the commissary to shop for groceries—better prices and broader selection were welcome benefits. He and I had always had the kind of relationship that allowed total, brutal honesty about any and all subjects. On one of our trips to the base we were talking about trust, honesty, and relationships and I made the statement that if I ever had sex again the man would have to be certified; meaning tested for any and all STD's, etc. The following week, he called to ask if I needed anything from the base but since we had shopped the week prior, I had no need. Since he saw a doctor on base, I assumed he had a regular check-up appointment. When he came back by for a sandwich he told me he had given his doctor my number to call since he quite often was out of range on his cell phone. He said it would be a few weeks before he expected to hear from the tests he had done. As it turned out he had asked his doctor to order a complete testing for STD's, etc. since his ex-wife had obviously been exposed to some of those possibilities while being involved in various affairs. When his doctor did call, about 3 weeks later, he asked for Seaborn (Gene's given first name) and the one recognized by the military. I said he was unavailable. The doctor then, asked for me. When I identified myself he gave the following message: "Tell Seaborn that all his tests are A-OK!" Little did I know that this sweet man was ready for more of a relationship than we currently had. We continue to say that had we known earlier what we know now, our relationship would have become intimate much earlier than it did. I remain grateful to God for saving the best for last. I am so completely spoiled and enjoying my life more than I ever dreamed possible.

# NUMEROLOGY

Love endures only when the lovers love many things together and not merely each other. My husband Gene and I have so many things in common that it surprises even us when we add a new one to our list.

I know nothing of numerology but a lot about numbers. I'll list a few commonalities that he and I shared long before we met. My marriage to Allen, my first husband, and Gene's mother's birthday were on November 27, 1965 and 1913, respectively. December 18 was the marriage anniversary of his parents and my parents, as well as the death date of my mother. Gene and I both had first marriages that lasted for 13 years and second marriages that lasted 22 years. He and I were both divorced in October, his on October 25, 2002 and mine on October 28, 1997. We both drove 1996 Oldsmobiles, almost identical in color. Our birthdays are on the 17th day of the month—his in November and mine in March.

As his sister Betty said when we told her we were getting married, "How many more signs do you need? DUH!"

The only constant in my life is change. Most of which is wonderful beyond description, but some, I could just as well do without. I have always thought that we have two choices: 1) greeting each day being afraid of everything we can't control or, 2) Opening ourselves to whatever might be around the corner. Chance encounters can surprise us, enlighten us, or change us forever.

People like me who write about lust and love as well as fiction and nonfiction and who have made several absolutely necessary detours in their lives; people who have more than one wedding ring in their jewelry boxes; have had enough experiences to be able to share some very valuable insights.

After 68 years of being a person and 40 years of being a wife, I've learned that when love comes your way, all you can do is close your eyes and open your arms. This time, I married for all the right reasons. We are each what the other had hoped for.

My sweet husband, Gene, is quick to tell others that I would not set the wedding date because I was too busy so he set a date for December 12, 2005, and I was certainly ready. I immediately began planning a small winter wonderland wedding and he very quickly announced that he already had planned everything. He is the only person I've ever trusted enough to allow them to make important decisions for me. He makes every effort to simplify my life and this has allowed my perfectionist personality to relax.

On the morning of our marriage, we drove to the Dale County courthouse and were married in the chambers of a wonderful red-headed lady judge. I love and appreciate my husband more each day. Liking him is a given—with his easy going nature and fun loving personality. Gene and I are very similar in values, attitudes, beliefs, backgrounds and intellect—so much so that being together is easy. We do not always agree but we always agree on the important things. After having lived with our former spouses, we probably both deserve Nobel peace prizes. There is none of that tension and dissention in our marriage. We work together 24/7 and are always committed to the task at hand. We accept each other's strengths and weaknesses and together we make an awesome team. We never take the other for granted but have a generous appreciation for each other. We are secure and unthreatened in our trust of each other. His love lifts me up; it makes me better than I was before. Miles do not separate us. My partner does romantic things like folding the laundry, sweeping the floor, drawing my bath, and holding my hand. He makes me laugh. He is a jewel more precious than any stone nature can create. On my husband's insistence, I stopped coloring my hair. Little did I know what freedom this would unfurl in me. I don't want or need to alter myself anymore. I want to be happy as I am—with who I am and what I have.

When I prayed for balance in my life, I had no idea how to attain that. My totally *Type A personality*, workaholic controller of all things has been transformed into a *Type A minus personality* (some of that I still cannot release) to a very easy going person who tries to control only myself. The perfectionism that frustrated me so much in the first 50 years of my life has now become gracious acceptance of most things. What a wonderful relief is the gift I've given myself! My family has always thought that I was born 100 years too late or too early. Chinette and paper napkins have now replaced the fine china, crystal, and linen that I thought was absolutely necessary in days past. The bed linen being changed weekly rather than every other day is perfectly acceptable. Seven course dinners have become sandwiches, or soups, or carryout. The dishes in the sink can actually stay there until tomorrow or until I am ready to do them. The world continues to spin and I am so happy to be taking this trip.

God did save the best for last! My Gene is the only person on this earth with whom I have truly shared my life. He enables me by being the best helpmate in the world. Together, with God's help, we can do anything. And we do! His strengths offset my weaknesses and together we are complete. I often tell him that I was just fine before he came into my life but should something happen to him, I'll never be fine again. He has spoiled me so and I think I have spoiled him in return. He is the husband I have always dreamed of—just never imagined his becoming a reality. I love him not just for the big things he does but for the million little things he does.

# DO WHAT YOU LOVE—LOVE WHAT YOU DO

My fun philosophy has been developing only in the last few years. I have decided that life is lived in reverse order. One should be born with enough money to get a good education, travel the world, enjoy the fun things of life while young enough and healthy enough to do so. Then, at about 50, when we suddenly become much wiser, we should start working and work until we die. We will be smart by this time and will have such wonderful life lessons and memories to share and to carry with us.

Travel, to me, is the best education one can have. It makes our world so much larger and when we see how other cultures and nationalities live, it broadens our horizons tremendously. It also makes us more grateful for the blessings we have.

Had anyone told me years ago that I could make a living as an artist, I never would have believed them. When I asked God to give me a gift, he did just that. I realized long ago that artists are not unique; we simply see things in a different light. And that light is a gift from God. I awoke one morning in June, 1993, with the idea of creating notecards embellished with pressed flowers. And, again, I made a promise to God that if he gave me a gift that I would give it my all and do my best to please Him. We both kept our word and Nature's Notables has been a blessing to me and my clients. From those simple notecards which I began creating have evolved very intricate compositions using pressed flowers from special life events—births, weddings, and funerals. Some typical examples of my works are shown on the following page.

*visit <u>www.naturesnotables.com</u> for more*

After preserving flowers from one's high school beauty pageant to one's wedding to the births of their children to the deaths of their parents, I develop treasured friendships with my clients.

It is not uncommon to meet and become friends with entire families through my work. It gives me the opportunity to see people at the highest and lowest points in their lives, to see their raw emotion. Grief counseling is an ever evolving opportunity for me. Our environment here at Rural Home offers a peaceful respite to those we serve. Again, all of this has evolved over several years and not by my doing but by divine intervention. Ours is a business that has literally grown itself. I never tire of my work and find that it feeds my soul.

Times change and people change, and so does the definition of success. All too often the corporate trappings of success: a six figure salary, promotions and respect within an industry, leave many feeling unfulfilled. Parts of the formula for fulfillment are flexibility and creativity. When one is truly fulfilled, they will see and be more grateful for their many blessings. When work excites and elates us, we no longer have a job to do but sheer pleasure to enjoy!

I learned that by not allowing others to set limits for me that I've been able to make a fair living doing something I love and that probably could not be done by following the rules of others. Few people have more tenacity than I and my *can do* spirit has taught me that if something doesn't work on the first try, that does not mean it can't be done. It simply has meant that I need to try another approach. By following my intuition and allowing things to unfold as I've gone, I have been able to develop a totally unique process of pressing flowers. No chemicals, colorants or additives touch the flowers in my artwork, from beginning to the end product.

If anyone else can do a thing, I can do it better. By increasing belief in ourselves, we can succeed at whatever we attempt. An old lady I knew in my childhood stated that *the only thing that makes a failure is not trying*. That statement is so true!

My creativity comes from my inner spirit. I really don't know what the end result will be when I'm composing a piece of artwork. I can teach others the technique of flower pressing but they must have an eye for color and a lot of confidence. Artists are not different; they simply see things differently. But in the right light, at the right time, everything is extraordinary. God created me to add to life on this earth. About twenty years or so ago, God gave me a grand gift when he hit me over the head with the idea of Nature's Notables. I try to create artwork for His glory on a daily basis.

# HOME

Many wonderful memories come to mind when we think of home. Homes come in many shapes and sizes and home is much more than a place; it is experiences, situations, and circumstances. We dream of a particular place we lived when all was right with the world and in our lives.

But, home is elusive. We seem to be trying to return to that wonderful memory or dream spot. Sometimes we strive to be somewhere we've been or want to go. Home then becomes our past or our future. We long for what was or will be the ideal where we are loved, where we belong and where we are not judged.

After Mother's Alzheimer's advanced to the point that she was disoriented most of the time, she always wanted to go *home*. When I would take her there, she still wanted to go *home*. I could not know because she could not communicate which home she wanted. Was it her childhood home, one of her homes during her adulthood, or her heavenly home? I will never know because we never found it.

There is no place like home and when we walk in our door, my husband and I, in unison, give a sigh of relief. It feels good, it smells good, and is the best place either of us has ever been. When we are in a contented, happy state of mind, a pup tent in the woods could feel like home. However, if things are not right in our world, the most majestic mansion cannot embrace us.

After looking at about twenty homes for sale and not finding a single one that I really liked, I had begun to wonder if I'd ever find a house to make into a home again. The moment I entered the front door of our present place, I knew I needed to look no further. Even though all the windows were heavily draped, the walls were all a dirty golden yellow color and the floors were covered with thirty year old gold wool carpet, I immediately saw the potential of this house. After ripping out the carpet and having the original heart pine floors refinished, I knew I was on the right track. Once the drapes were down and the walls painted stark white, I really began to feel at home and to feel a peace I had not known in many years. There are very special places in all our lives and our homes should be near the top of that list.

A thirteen hundred year old cathedral in Ulm, Germany, will always hold a unique spot in my heart. One rainy, dreary November morning in 1991, I had the unique privilege of standing alone in the sanctuary of that church. By alone, I mean that not another human being was visible to me. But, I felt such a strong spirit there that I knew I was in the company of my Supreme Being. I had heard others allude to epiphanies but could only imagine of what they spoke. Now I know. In a matter of minutes I became a new person. My entire being changed. I felt different. I thought different thoughts. I knew that my life was about to change drastically and that I could do whatever was required of me. From that day forward, I have been the most blessed person on earth. There are those places in each of our lives that stir within us a renewed sense of self and empower us to look beyond what we are and to discover who we can be.

# RESIDENT GHOST

While my house was being refurbished, I lived here or should say more accurately, camped out amongst the unpacked boxes. My bed was set up so I could at least sleep here, while remodeling the house. Each day when the painter would come, the bed served as a place to stack things which were in his way. There were nights when I was too exhausted to unload all the stuff from my bed so I'd make room on one side, just large enough for my weary body, and sleep with boxes and whatever happened to have been placed on the other side for safekeeping. On one of those nights I was awakened from a deep sleep by a burning sensation in my nose. The smell of cherry pipe tobacco was overwhelming in my bedroom. I simply laid there trying to figure from whence had come this very strong odor. Several evenings later, the granddaughter of the original owner of the house came out to have dinner and as we sat around the dining table afterwards, we heard a creak on the stairs. She immediately said, "Come on down and join us, Parke." We laughed as she was explaining that her grandfather had been a very disciplined, habitual person who did everything on a very predictable schedule. Nine-thirty to ten p.m. was his standard bedtime so she suggested that the creak could have been caused by his climbing the stairs to go to bed. I told her of my tobacco smoke incident a few nights earlier and she informed me that her grandfather soaked his cigars in amaretto—therefore the cherry smell. There have been dozens of times when that same smell has permeated the house. The timing of his visits, in retrospect, seems very significant on many of those occasions.

After my husband's prostate cancer surgery, on his first night home from the hospital, he had a half hour visit from the Resident Ghost. His presence is very comforting. On my sister's last visit (we had no way of knowing it would be her final visit) as she and her husband were going to their car to drive back to Louisiana, she stopped in the front doorway because she too, smelled the cherry pipe tobacco. We then shared with her that we are blessed by his presence and that we *smell* him rather than *see* him. My sister had a malignant brain tumor and died before being able to visit again.

When we were getting ready for our first cookbook expo, my niece was assisting with last minute details the evening before the big party. She asked my husband who was in the barn, and he said, "No one". She assured him that she had just seen a lady run through the barn. My husband saw a strange lady in our kitchen just a few weeks ago.

We had a rat terrier, Precious, who was very attuned to our ghost. On occasion, I would have to go upstairs and bring her back down in my arms. She and Ghost must have been playing a wonderful game because she simply ignored me when I commanded her to return downstairs. Some of Parke's descendants have told me that his favorite dog breed was the rat terrier and that through the years he had owned several of them. When this type of information is revealed after the fact, it certainly makes one wonder at the coincidence.

There is a particular spot, down one of our lanes, that is very cool, probably 65 degrees, even on the hottest day of the year. My husband and I go there often on scorching days and sit on the golf cart, just enjoying the respite from the heat. It feels almost as though there is a breeze blowing there.

In years past, there were many farm laborers who lived in shacks on this property. Surely, there were many births and deaths during that time. The large Pennsylvania Dutch style barn is, according to our barn painter, the largest of its type south of Kentucky. In its earlier years, it was used to house hogs, cows, mules, and horses. The original owners farmed a few thousand acres of cotton, corn, peanuts, and pastures and bred livestock of such fine quality that they won national awards. From what I've been told, the original owners were leaders in the community, both socially and financially. It is a pleasure to reside in a home that enjoys such a rich history. We hope to leave it an even better place than when we arrived.

# CHRIST, OUR HOPE

He is our only hope! Until we each look inward and do what we can, in our small ways, to make this a better world, all the money and all the power will make no difference. Being the most blessed person in the world helps me to realize God's love and grace have been the one and only true constant in my life. He has given me stability and comfort when my heart has been broken and disappointments have abounded. He has given me the courage to do what was right even when my stubborn self-will and temptations surrounded me. My God and I have daily conversations—an ongoing dialogue, which is non-frightening and very friendly.

I think that He has been generous to me because of my attitude. After leaving Rex, I continued to pray for him and his well-being. My friends have often questioned my sanity because I have no malice or hatred for him. He has my pity and sorrow for the wasted blessings in his life. My heart hurts for him for *what might have been.*

I believe that the moral values of our forefathers must be re-instated, enforced, and certainly respected in order to reverse our country's direction. The reward for laziness is welfare. Self-esteem in children is not built by neglecting to discipline them. Vulgarity, profanity, and pornography are not the intended freedoms of expression. Political power should not be a license to steal the future of our generation and those that, hopefully, will follow.

In the midst of life's uncertainties in the days ahead, I do know that I have the certainty of His love. And, as I look back, I thank Him for His goodness to me—far beyond what I deserved. I hope to live life fully today and ask His guidance while looking forward to tomorrow. I pray often for that happy spot between too much and too little.